ACCESS AWARD IN ACCOUNTING SOFTWARE

STUDY TEXT 2018

Qualifications and Credit Framework

AAT Level 1

British Library Cataloguing-in-Publication Data

A catalogue record for this book is available from the British Library.

Published by
Kaplan Publishing UK
Unit 2, The Business Centre
Molly Millars Lane
Wokingham
Berkshire
RG41 2QZ

ISBN 978 1 78740 037 5

Printed and bound in Great Britain.

Kaplan Publishing would like to thank Angela Renshaw and Deborah Seed for their contributions towards the production of this publication.

CONTENTS

INTRODUCTION

HOW TO USE THESE MATERIALS

These Kaplan Publishing learning materials have been carefully designed to make your learning experience as easy as possible and to give you the best chance of success in your AAT assessments.

They contain a number of features to help you in the study process.

The sections on the Unit Guide, the Assessment and Study Skills should be read before you commence your studies.

They are designed to familiarise you with the nature and content of the assessment and to give you tips on how best to approach your studies.

STUDY TEXT

This Study Text has been specially prepared for the revised AAT Access qualification introduced in 2018.

It is written in a practical and interactive style by expert classroom tutors.

In this Study Text:

- key terms and concepts are clearly defined

- all topics are illustrated with practical examples with clearly worked solutions based on sample tasks provided by the AAT in the new assessment style

- frequent activities throughout and at the end of the chapters ensure that what you have learnt is regularly reinforced

- 'Test your understanding' activities are included within each chapter to apply your learning and develop your understanding

- a 'Case Study' brings the subject to life and puts the content covered into a real life context

- Mock Assessments and end of chapter activities reinforce understanding to prepare you for the assessment.

ICONS

The chapters include the following icons throughout.

They are designed to assist you in your studies by identifying key definitions and the points at which you can test yourself on the knowledge gained.

Definition

These sections explain important areas of Knowledge which must be understood and reproduced in an assessment

Example

The illustrative examples can be used to help develop an understanding of topics before attempting the activity exercises

Test your understanding

These are exercises which give the opportunity to assess your understanding of all the assessment areas.

Case study

These examples put the chapter content into a real life context, using the case study of Chrissie Norris and her role at TotalPhoto Ltd.

Case study activities

Following the chapter summary, these questions enable further practice using the real life context of the above case study.

KAPLAN PUBLISHING

UNIT GUIDE

Introduction

The AAT Access Award in Accounting Software offers students at Level 1 the opportunity to develop their skills in using accounting software. This qualification can offer a route into employment, support students in their existing work, or help students to pursue further study with AAT.

This qualification will particularly suit those students who have had minimal work experience or those who need some additional support in order to progress. This may include younger learners seeking tangible and finance-specific skills, adults seeking to validate their existing skills in order to enter into or progress in their career, or students who would like to test their abilities before progressing further with AAT.

Students should choose the AAT Access Award in Accounting Software if they wish to focus on specific technical skills in using accounting software. Students completing this qualification may wish to pursue careers in finance or business in either the private or public sectors. This qualification complements the other qualifications in the suite of AAT Access qualifications and may be combined with the AAT Access Award in Bookkeeping to lay a strong foundation for further study with AAT in either accountancy or bookkeeping.

The skills developed in this qualification can lead to employment in junior or supporting administrative roles in companies across a wide range of public and private sectors, for example, as a:

- trainee bookkeeper
- data entry clerk
- accounts administrator
- invoice entry administrator
- payments administrator.

Overview and learning outcomes

Overview

The AAT Access Award in Accounting Software introduces students to the use of accounting software. The qualification covers a range of skills and the relevant supporting knowledge in one mandatory unit:

• Access to Accounting Software (45 guided learning hours).

Accounting software is now widely used in most organisations. This unit introduces students to using accounting software and the main features of accounting software. On completion of this unit, students will be able to set up general ledger accounts and to record bank and cash transactions from a variety of documents, including bank statements. They will be able to recognise potential risks to accounting software security and know how to protect accounting software against threats. Students will be able to use accounting software to produce a variety of reports for a business, such as a trial balance and an audit trail.

Students will also explore the differences between cloud accounting software and traditional accounting software.

Most students will benefit from gaining an understanding of manual bookkeeping before studying this unit. This may be gained through the AAT Access Award in Bookkeeping.

Learning outcomes

The Access Award in Accounting Software comprises of four learning outcomes:

1. Understand the benefits and risks of using accounting software

2. Set up accounts

3. Record bank and cash transactions

4. Produce reports using accounting software

Scope of content and assessment criteria

ix

1. Understand the benefits and risks of using accounting software (Chapter 2)

1.1 Features of accounting software compared to manual bookkeeping

Students need to know:

- features of accounting software that allow increased speed and automation:
  - report processing
  - data input
  - batch processing
- 'ease of use' features commonly included in accounting software:
  - integrated software
  - tools and wizards
  - help functions
  - different report layouts (charts, tables)
- benefits of being able to import and export data to and from other programs:
  - to work with data more flexibly
  - save time
  - reduce risk of human error
  - communicate information in various formats
- advantages of reports that may be produced in accounting software:
  - real-time financial position
  - analysis of income and expenses.

1.2 . Advantages and disadvantages to users of different types of accounting software

Students need to know:

- comparison of 'off the shelf' versus bespoke software:
  - cost
  - levels of support for users
  - timeframe for development
  - range of functions used by business
  - frequency and ease of updates
  - level of training required to use software
  - type of subscription

- comparison of traditional accounting software versus cloud software:
    - cost
    - levels of support for users
    - range of functions used by business
    - frequency and ease of updates
    - upgrade capacity
    - level of training required to use software
    - access from multiple devices
    - type of subscription
    - access to internet.

1.3 Accounting software security

Students need to know:

- potential threats to data security:
    - viruses
    - hacking
    - phishing
    - system crashes
    - employee fraud
    - corrupt files
    - natural disasters (flood, fire)
    - accidental deletion
- how to protect accounting software against threats:
    - access rights
    - passwords
    - encryption
    - firewalls
    - secure backups.

2. Set up accounts (Chapter 4)

2.1 Create new accounts in the general ledger

Students need to know:

- how to process assets, liabilities, income, expenses, capital and drawings in accounting software.

Students must be able to:

- select accounts from the default list of accounts provided by the software

- add new accounts to the default list of accounts provided by the software where that account name is not included in the default list
- enter the date and amount of an opening balance, including nil balances.

2.2 Amend existing account names in the general ledger
Students must be able to:

- amend account names used in the default list of accounts provided by the software.

3. Record bank and cash transactions (Chapters 1 & 8)

3.1 Accounting terminology
Students must be able to:
- differentiate between expenses, drawings and assets
- differentiate between income, capital introduced and liabilities.

3.2 Record transactions from a bank statement
Students must be able to:
- record payments from a bank statement entering:
    - date
    - amount
    - general ledger code (classification of expense, asset)
- record receipts from a bank statement entering:
    - date
    - amount
    - general ledger code (classification of bank interest, sales or cash account transfer)
- know how to process VAT-inclusive (standard rated only) and VAT-exclusive amounts in accounting software.

3.3 Record cash transactions
Students must be able to:
- record cash payments from source documents entering:
    - date
    - amount (net, VAT and total)
    - general ledger code (classification of expense, drawings or bank transfer)

- record cash receipts entering:
  - date
  - amount (net, VAT and total)
  - general ledger code (classification of sales type or capital introduced)
- process VAT-inclusive (standard rated only) and VAT-exclusive amounts in accounting software.

4. Produce reports using accounting software (Chapter 9)

4.1 Reports that may be produced using accounting software

Students need to know:

- types of reports:
  - trial balance
  - audit trail at the end of a period
  - sales analysis for a specified time period
  - expenses analysis for a specified time period
  - all general ledger accounts or specific general ledger accounts only
- the importance of ensuring that all information required is processed in the system before a report is produced.

4.2 Produce reports using accounting software

Students must be able to:

- produce reports:
  - trial balance at the end of a period
  - audit trail at the end of a period
  - bank payments analysis for a specified time period
  - bank receipts analysis for a specified time period
  - sales analysis for a specified time period
  - expenses analysis for a specified time period
  - all general ledger accounts or specific general ledger accounts only.

The assessment   xiii

The assessment for this unit will require students to upload evidence to the assessment platform in one or more of the formats specified: XLS, XLSX, CSV, PDF. Students should allow a minimum of 15 minutes within the full assessment time to upload their evidence. If evidence is not submitted within this time, the evidence will not be marked.

The assessment will be under timed conditions. The timed allowed for the assessment is 2 hours.

The assessment is partially computer-marked and partially human-marked.

The weighting of the learning outcomes is as follows:

1.	Understand the benefits and risks of using accounting software 20%	
2.	Set up accounts	25%
3.	Record bank and cash transactions	35%
4.	Produce reports using accounting software	20%
Total		100%

STUDY SKILLS

Preparing to study

Devise a study plan

Determine which times of the week you will study.

Split these times into sessions of at least one hour for study of new material. Any shorter periods could be used for revision or practice.

Put the times you plan to study onto a study plan for the weeks from now until the assessment and set yourself targets for each period of study – in your sessions make sure you cover the whole course, activities and the associated questions with answers at the back of the Study Text.

When working through your course, compare your progress with your plan and, if necessary, re-plan your work (perhaps including extra sessions) or, if you are ahead, do some extra revision/practice questions.

Effective studying

Active reading

You are not expected to learn the text by rote, rather, you must understand what you are reading and be able to use it to pass the assessment and develop good practice.

A good technique is to use SQ3Rs – Survey, Question, Read, Recall, Review:

1 Survey the chapter

Look at the headings and read the introduction, knowledge, skills and content, so as to get an overview of what the chapter deals with.

2 Question

Whilst undertaking the survey ask yourself the questions you hope the chapter will answer for you.

3 Read

Read through the chapter thoroughly working through the activities and, at the end, making sure that you can meet the learning objectives shown within the summary.

4 Recall

At the end of each chapter, try to recall the main ideas of the section/chapter without referring to the text. This is best done after short break of a couple of minutes after the reading stage.

5 Review

Check that your recall notes are correct.

You may also find it helpful to re-read the chapter to try and see the topic(s) it deals with as a whole.

Note taking

Taking notes is a useful way of learning, but do not simply copy out the text. The notes must:

- be in your own words
- be concise
- cover the key points
- be well organised
- be modified as you study further chapters in this text or in related ones.

Trying to summarise a chapter without referring to the text can be a useful way of determining which areas you know and which you don't.

Three ways of taking notes

1   **Summarise the key points of a chapter**

2   **Make linear notes**

A list of headings, subdivided with sub-headings listing the key points.

If you use linear notes, you can use different colours to highlight key points and keep topic areas together.

Use plenty of space to make your notes easy to use.

3   **Try a diagrammatic form**

The most common of which is a mind map.

To make a mind map, put the main heading in the centre of the paper and put a circle around it.

Draw lines radiating from this to the main sub-headings which again have circles around them.

Continue the process from the sub-headings to sub-sub-headings.

Highlighting and underlining

You may find it useful to underline or highlight key points in your study text – but do be selective.

You may also wish to make notes in the margins.

Further reading

In addition to this text, you should also read the 'Student section' of the 'Accounting Technician' magazine every month to keep abreast of any guidance from the examiners.

Basic accounting terminology

1

Introduction

This Study Text will guide you through the key aspects of computerised accounting and ways that accounting software is used in the workplace.

The purpose of accounting is to be able to provide financial information about an organisation. For example, managers will want to keep track of the profit made by the organisation in a certain period, and they will also want to see how much the organisation is worth at a specific point in time.

To be able to provide this information it is important that the business transactions of the organisation are recorded and summarised into accounting records.

This chapter will introduce you to the accounting terminology used to record these business transactions. You will also be introduced to a case study of a fictitious company called TotalPhoto Ltd, which will be used throughout the Study Text as the basis for activities.

KNOWLEDGE	CONTENTS
Record bank and cash transactions 3.1 Accounting terminology	1 Assets and liabilities 2 Income and expenditure 3 Cash and credit transactions 4 Profit and loss 5 Capital and drawings 6 Summary and further questions

1 Assets and liabilities

1.1 Case study: an introduction

> ### 📖 Case study
>
> TotalPhoto Ltd is a small company based in the market town of Miltonby in Lancashire. It is owned by two directors, Matt Evans and Stuart Lincoln.
>
> TotalPhoto Ltd. was established in 2015 when both Matt and Stuart left Art College. As the company has grown, they have employed an accounting apprentice called Chrissie Norris, who is responsible for processing the day to day financial transactions of the business.
>
> Chrissie knows only too well the importance of accurate bookkeeping. She is an excellent student, thorough in all that she does.
>
> As the company move to using a computerised accounting package, they want to ensure that Chrissie is using the correct terminology for each task so they can be sure that she is inputting the financial information accurately into the accounting system.
>
> Make sure that you do the activities set for Chrissie within this chapter.

1.2 What is an asset?

Assets are items of value which an organisation owns in order to generate profit by selling goods or providing a service.

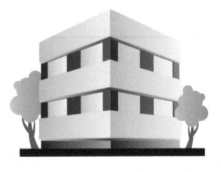

Assets can be physical such as cash, land, buildings etc. or non-physical such as copyrights, trademarks and patents. Either way, an asset is something that a company acquires to help increase its value or to improve its overall operations.

> ### 🔍 Definition
>
> **An asset** is an item of value owned by an organisation.

1.3 Different types of asset

> ### 💡 Examples
>
> Assets include:
>
> **Premises** – organisations usually need a building from which to carry out their business. These premises could be an office building, a shop, or a factory.
>
> **Fixtures and fittings** – these are items in the premises which are used to provide goods or services. For example, the computers in an office, the shelving in a shop, or machinery in a factory.
>
> **Vehicles** – vehicles may be needed to deliver goods or provide a service to customers.
>
> **Inventory** – goods which are ready to sell to customers are kept in stock
>
> **Bank** – the funds available in the organisation's bank account may be used to purchase more stock to sell.
>
> **Cash** – some organisations keep money on the premises so that they can buy small items.
>
> **Trade Receivables** – amounts owed to the organisation by customers as a result of sales made on credit.
>
> **Copyrights** – a legal right which protects any work created by an organisation. It prevents others from using it or distributing it without their permission
>
> **Trademarks** – the brand, logo or slogan of an organisation which helps to distinguish it from another organisation. For example, Tesco is a 'brand'. Nobody would be allowed to set up a shop of their own and call it Tesco, as the name belongs to them.
>
> **Patents** – if an organisation invents a new product, they may apply for a patent from the government which stops others for a limited period of time from creating, using or selling it without their permission.

1.4 What is a liability?

A liability is an amount of money that an organisation owes to a supplier, bank or other lender. An organisation will have a legal obligation to pay back the money that they owe. The money will usually have been used to buy assets for the organisation to use.

Total liabilities are deducted from total assets to calculate an organisation's worth at a specific period in time.

🔍 Definition

A liability is a debt owed by an organisation to other organisations, businesses and individuals.

1.5 Different types of liability

💡 Examples

Liabilities include:

Payables – amounts owed by the organisation to suppliers of goods and services.

Bank Overdraft – an arrangement that allows an organisation to take more money out of its bank than it has put in. The money is owed to the bank on a short-term basis.

Bank Loan – a fixed amount of money an organisation borrows from the bank usually over a longer period of time.

📝 Test your understanding 1

Chrissie had to classify the following as an asset or a liability to be able to identify them accurately within the system.

Classify them accurately by putting a tick in the correct box.

	Asset	Liability
Machinery		
A bank loan		
A bank overdraft		
Inventory		
Receivables		
Payables		
A patent		

KAPLAN PUBLISHING

2 Income and expenditure

2.1 Introduction

The purpose of most organisations is to make a profit or to raise funds so that they can continue supplying goods and services to customers. To calculate profit, **expenditure** is deducted from **income**.

2.2 What is income?

Any money received from the supply of goods and services to customers is known as income.

2.3 What is expenditure?

Any money paid for purchasing the goods and services and day to day expenses is known as expenditure.

🔍 Definitions

Income is the money received by an organisation from selling its goods and services.

Expenditure is the money paid by an organisation to purchase goods and services.

📝 Test your understanding 2

Chrissie needs to classify the following as income or expenditure to be able to identify them accurately within the system. Classify them accurately by putting a tick in the correct box.

	Income	Expenditure
Payments to suppliers		
Electricity bill		
The cost of goods and services		
Cash sales		
Sales of services		
Telephone bill		
Water bill		

---

3 Cash and credit transactions

3.1 Recording cash and credit transactions

Income is the amount of money received by an organisation from the sale of its goods or services. Returning to our case study, TotalPhoto Ltd sell cameras, photograph packages and accessories to their customers; these would be classified as their sales of goods. They also have a help desk that offer advice on technical issues; this would be classified as their sales of services.

Income is the amount of money received by an organisation from its sales. Sometimes the money is received immediately, this is called a **cash sale.** Sometimes the money is received later, this is called a **credit sale**. It is important that cash and credit transactions are recorded separately so that the organisation knows how much money it is owed by customers, and how much it owes to suppliers.

3.2 Cash and credit sales

🔍 Definitions

Sales is the exchange of goods or services to an individual or organisation in exchange for money.

A **customer** is an individual or organisation to whom the goods or services have been sold. The organisation supplying the goods or services will then receive money in exchange.

A **trade receivable (also known as a debtor)** is a customer who has been sold goods on credit and who owes the business the money in respect of the sale.

Cash Sales is the term used to describe a payment at point of sale. The payment itself can be made by cash (currency), cheque, debit or credit card, or bank transfer. An example of a cash sale is when you go into a shop, choose the items you want to buy, and pay for them immediately.

Credit Sales are sales made where the goods or services will be paid later than the point of sale. Many organisations give credit to their regular trade customers so that one payment can be made for all the transactions made in each month. Credit sales are usually recorded by way of an invoice which will be covered in a later chapter.

KAPLAN PUBLISHING

3.3 Cash and credit customers

With cash sales the organisation gets the money immediately from the customer and the relationship ends there. With credit customers, there is a risk to the organisation that the customer may not pay for the goods.

Therefore, before allowing customers to pay on credit the organisation will make certain checks to ensure that the customer can pay. If these checks identify that the customer has the ability to pay its debts, payment terms will be agreed with the customer and a credit account set up.

Payment terms usually state the length of time a customer has to pay for their goods and also a maximum amount that they are allowed to owe the business at any one time. The amounts outstanding from customers can be analysed so that a business can see at what point they can expect the money to come into their bank account.

If customers are taking longer to pay than expected, a business should chase for the outstanding monies to ensure a continual flow of cash moving through the organisation.

It is assumed that the money owed by credit customers will be paid and therefore they are classed as **trade receivables or receivables**. Receivables have the ability to be converted into cash and are therefore classed as assets of the organisation.

Test your understanding 3

Chrissie has been asked to identify whether the following TotalPhoto Ltd transactions would be classified as a cash or credit transaction?

Put a tick in the correct box.

	Cash	Credit
A customer purchases a camera and pays by credit card		
A customer buys a personalised photo package and pays by debit card		
A customer buys 5 lenses for professional use, and pays in 30 days		

3.4 Cash and credit purchases

> **Q** **Definition**
>
> **Purchases** – to buy goods or services from an organisation in exchange for money.

Cash Purchases are when goods or services are paid for at the time of purchase.

> **Case study**
>
> How Two Ltd may purchase some stock and pay by 'cash'. Although the payment could be by cash (currency), credit card or debit card or bank transfer, if the payment is made immediately it is classed as a cash purchase.

Credit Purchases are when an organisation pays for the goods or services sometime after making the purchase. The money will be sent to the supplier after an agreed amount of time, for example, thirty days.

The supplier is now a payable of the organisation and as money is owed to the supplier in respect of the transaction, they are classed as a liability of the business.

> **Q** **Definition**
>
> A **supplier** is an individual or organisation providing goods or services to another in exchange for money.
>
> A **trade payable** is a supplier who is owed money for goods purchased on credit.

> **Test your understanding 4**
>
> Fill in the gaps below to complete the sentences. Choose from the Pick list provided.
>
> When an organisation pays for items of expenditure at the time of purchase this is known as a _____
>
> When an organisation allows a customer to pay the amount they owe at a later date this is known as a _____
>
> **Pick List**
>
> credit sale   cash sale   cash purchase   credit purchase.

📝 Test your understanding 5

Match the definition with the correct term.

Terms	Definition
Payable	Something the business owns
Receivable	A person or another business that the organisation owes money to
Asset	Something the business owes
Liability	A person or another business that owes money to the organisation

---

📝 Test your understanding 6

Chrissie has been asked to identify whether the following TotalPhoto Ltd transactions would be classified as a cash or credit transaction?

Put a tick in the correct box.

	Cash	Credit
Matt purchases some photographic films online and pays by bank transfer		
Stuart buys some display albums and is issued an invoice from the supplier		
Chrissie purchases a computer and pays by credit card		

📝 Test your understanding 7

C Froome's Cycle World

Mr Froome has a small shop selling and repairing bicycles for individual customers.

He buys the spare parts that he needs from a large wholesaler.

Do you think that Mr Froome's income comes from cash sales or credit sales?

Do you think that the expenditure for spare parts is cash purchases or credit purchases?

3.5 The Cash Book and Petty Cash Book

The word 'cash' is also used in accounting as a name for recording monetary transactions.

A **Cash Book** is used to keep a record of most of the receipts of income and payments of expenses made by the organisation. The actual monies received and recorded may be by cash (currency), cheque, credit card or debit card, or bank transfer.

A **Petty Cash Book** is used to record small amounts of cash that most businesses hold in order to make small cash payments regularly. Petty cash systems and the management of petty cash are addressed further, later in this book.

4 Profit and loss

4.1 What is a profit or loss?

A business needs to make money in order to operate. By selling goods or services they generate income, from this they need to deduct their expenses for buying in those goods and services. This is called the 'profit' or 'loss'.

In order for a business to generate a 'profit', their income needs to be more than their expenses. If their expenses are more than their income, they would make a loss which could make the business fail.

🔍 Definitions

Profit is the amount of money an organisation earns after expenditure has been deducted from income.

Loss is when an organisation has spent more money than it has earned from income.

4.2 What happens when a business makes a profit?

An organisation's main goal should be to make a profit. No business can survive long-term if they don't make a profit.

Profit is paid to the owners of a company or its shareholders. Alternatively, it can be used as a saving opportunity to enable the organisation to re-invest and therefore grow the business. Growing a business means expanding it; making it bigger. This may be through investing in research or new technology, opening new offices, operating in new markets or obtaining other businesses. A bigger company means a bigger part of the market share and therefore increased profitability.

4.3 What happens when a business makes a loss?

If a business is spending more on expenses than they are making from the sales of goods or services, they will be making a loss.

If an organisation is making a loss then the chances are that their bank account may become overdrawn. Ultimately, they will be charged high amounts of interest for this which only increases their expenditure even more. If this were to happen, the business may not have enough money to pay their suppliers which could result in the suppliers putting their account on hold, or even withdrawing their credit agreement.

As a result, the business would find it difficult to purchase goods or services for resale, meaning that they would struggle to meet their customer's demands. If this is the case, it can cause problems and the business could fail.

Test your understanding 8

Chrissie has been asked to identify which of the following are indicators of a business making a profit or a loss. Put a tick in the correct box.

	Profit	Loss
The business could fail		
The bank account is overdrawn		
A saving opportunity		
There is an opportunity for growth		
There is a high volume of sales		
Money has been invested in new ventures		
Not enough money to pay for purchases		
Suppliers withdraw their credit agreement		

Example

NB Solutions Ltd has recorded all sales income and expenditure for the previous month. Alba, the Accounts Assistant, has been asked to calculate the profit for the month.

	£
Sales income	125,000
Cost of sales	75,000
Wages	15,000
Premises expenses	3,000
Vehicle expenses	2,500

Solution:

To calculate **profit (or loss)** the cost of sales are deducted from the sales income.

	Sales income:	£125,000
−	Cost of sales	- £75,000
−	Wages	- £15,000
−	Premises expenses	- £3,000
−	Vehicle expenses	- £2,500
=	**Total Profit**	**£29,500**

Therefore, Alba can report a profit of £29,500 for the month.

Note: If Alba had ended up with a minus figure at the end of her calculation, she would know that the company had made a loss i.e. NB Solutions Ltd's expenses were more than the company's income.

Case study

In September, TotalPhoto recorded income from sales of £82,000. The cost of those sales was £66,000 and the other expenses were £25,000.

Chrissie is asked whether the company made a profit or a loss.

Solution:

	Sales income:	£82,000
−	Cost of sales	- £66,000
−	Other expenses	- £25,000
=		**-£9,000**

Their expenses are more than their income so TotalPhoto Ltd made a loss of £9,000 in September.

Test your understanding 9

To assess the performance of TotalPhoto Ltd's office in September, Chrissie looks at the figures from the previous month. In August, the company recorded income of £85,000. The cost of those sales was £69,000 and the other expenses were £18,000.

Did they make a profit or a loss? How do the two months compare?

Test your understanding 10

Chrissie has been asked to see if the performance of TotalPhoto Ltd is similar to its sister company in Scotland. The Scottish company has recorded all sales income and expenditure for the previous month.

Chrissie needs to calculate the profit or loss for the month given the following information:

	£
Sales income from cash and credit sales	78,000
Cost of sales	50,700
Wages	7,500
Premises expenses	1,750
Vehicle expenses	2,000

Test your understanding 11

Chrissie concludes that in some months, TotalPhoto Ltd has a total income lower than the costs of sales plus expenses.

Chrissie must look at this statement and then determine – has the company made a profit or a loss in those months? She must provide a brief explanation for her answer for one of the managers.

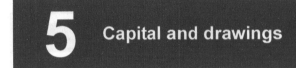

5 Capital and drawings

5.1 What is capital?

> 🔍 **Definition**
>
> **Capital** is the initial amount of money or assets that the owner of a business puts in to start it up. Essentially the business owes that money back to the owner and therefore it is classed as a **liability** of the business.

For example, if a person set up a taxi firm using £10,000 of their own money to fund the business, and they transferred their own car worth £10,000 into the business, this would equate to £20,000 capital for the business.

The owner of a business is completely separate from the business itself and therefore capital within a business is owed back to the owner. This means that capital is classified as a liability of the company.

5.2 What are drawings?

> 🔍 **Definition**
>
> **Drawings** is an amount of money that is taken out of the business by the owner of the business for their own personal use. Essentially the owner owes that money back to the business and therefore they are classed as an **asset** to the business.

Sometimes the owner will withdraw money from the business bank/cash account for purposes which are not intended for the business. Alternatively, they may take assets such as equipment or inventory for themselves, again this is classed as drawings.

Drawings reduce the amount of capital in a business and therefore it is important to account for them correctly within the bookkeeping system.

6 Summary and further questions

This chapter has introduced you to some important accounting terminology. You can distinguish between assets, liabilities, income and expenditure and looked at the difference between credit sales and purchases and cash sales and purchases.

Finally, the chapter looked at how the profit or loss of an organisation is calculated and you should understand that a business needs more income than expenses in order to operate profitably.

Let us now return to the case study for some further practice questions to test your knowledge of this key terminology.

Case study activity 1

Chrissie has been asked to define some key terms to help explain her e-mail to the managers. Choose the correct option in each statement:

a. The sum of money spent in making sales is known as [sales/cost of sales]

b. If total income is greater than the cost of sales plus other expenses the organisation has made a [profit/loss]

c. If total income is less than the cost of sales plus other expenses the organisation has made a [profit/loss]

Case study activity 2

Chrissie has been given a list of terms which are commonly used every day in her department. She needs to decide if they are assets, liabilities, income or expenditure? Put a tick in the correct box.

	Asset	Liability	Income	Expenditure
Creditors				
Electricity bill				
Money in the bank				
Bank overdraft				
Sales to customers				
Debtors				
Office computers				

Case study activity 3

Chrissie needs to decide whether the following TotalPhoto Ltd transactions are cash or credit sales, or cash or credit purchases? Put a tick in the correct box.

	Cash Sale	Credit Sale	Cash Purchase	Credit Purchase
Paper bought from a supplier and paid for immediately.				
Products delivered to a customer who will pay at the end of the month.				
Camera components bought from a supplier on credit.				
A payment received from a customer for goods purchased online and paid for at the checkout.				

Case study activity 4

Last month TotalPhoto Ltd's Head Office recorded income and expenditure in the table below:

Income and Expenditure	£
Sales	156,000
Cost of Sales	93,600
Wages	21,060
Administration Expenses	18,720
Selling Expenses	12,844

Chrissie needs to use the income and expenditure figures to calculate the profit or loss and state underneath whether this would be a profit or loss.

Profit / Loss: £

KAPLAN PUBLISHING

Case study activity 5

The following month's recorded income and expenditure is shown in the table below:

Income and Expenditure	£
Sales	152,880
Cost of Sales	91,728
Wages	20,640
Administration Expenses	18,350
Selling Expenses	12,590

Chrissie needs to use the income and expenditure figures to calculate the profit or loss and state underneath whether this would be a profit or loss.

Profit / Loss: £

Answers to chapter activities

Test your understanding 1

	Asset	Liability
Machinery	✓	
A bank loan		✓
A bank overdraft		✓
Inventory	✓	
Receivables	✓	
Payables		✓
A patent	✓	

Test your understanding 2

	Income	Expenditure
Payments to suppliers		✓
Electricity bill		✓
The cost of goods and services		✓
Cash sales	✓	
Sales of services	✓	
Telephone bill		✓
Water bill		✓

Test your understanding 3

	Cash	Credit
A customer purchases a camera and pays by credit card	✓	
A customer buys a personalised photo package and pays by debit card	✓	
A customer buys 5 lenses for professional use, and pays in 30 days		✓

Test your understanding 4

When an organisation pays for items of expenditure at the time of purchase this is known as a **cash purchase.**

When an organisation allows a customer to pay the amount they owe at a later date this is known as a **credit sale.**

Test your understanding 5

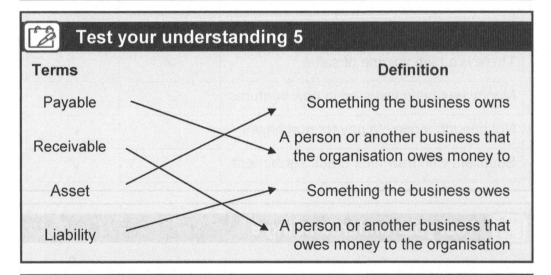

Terms	Definition
Payable	Something the business owns
Receivable	A person or another business that the organisation owes money to
Asset	Something the business owes
Liability	A person or another business that owes money to the organisation

Test your understanding 6

	Cash	Credit
Matt purchases some photographic films online and pays by bank transfer	✓	
Stuart buys some display albums and is issued an invoice from the supplier		✓
Chrissie purchases a computer and pays by credit card	✓	

Test your understanding 7

Mr Froome's income is most likely to be from cash sales. His customers are individuals who will probably pay when they come to pick up their bicycles. They are unlikely to be very regular customers.

His expenditure for the spare parts is likely to be a credit purchase. As Mr Froome will buy regularly from the supplier he may have been given credit so that he can make daily or weekly purchases and then pay for all he owes at a later date.

Test your understanding 8

	Profit	Loss
The business could fail		✓
The bank account is overdrawn		✓
A saving opportunity	✓	
There is an opportunity for growth	✓	
There is a high volume of sales	✓	
Money has been invested in new ventures	✓	
Not enough money to pay for purchases		✓
Suppliers withdraw their credit agreement		✓

Test your understanding 9

	£
Sales income	85,000
Cost of sales	-69,000
Other expenses	-18,000
	-2,000

This means that their sales income is lower than their expenses and therefore they have made **a loss of £2,000**.

Although this is a loss, it is £7,000 less than the loss in September.

Test your understanding 10

	£
Sales income	78,000
Cost of sales	-50,700
Wages	-7,500
Premises expenses	-1,750
Vehicle expenses	-2,000
	16,050

The company have made **a profit of £16,050** because their sales income is more than the total of their expenditure.

Test your understanding 11

As their sales income is lower than cost of sales plus expenses, the business has made a loss.

Case study activity 1

a. The sum of money spent in making sales is known as **cost of sales**
b. If total income is greater than the cost of sales plus other expenses the organisation has made a **profit**
c. If total income is less than the cost of sales plus other expenses the organisation has made a **loss**

Case study activity 2

	Asset	**Liability**	**Income**	**Expenditure**
Creditors		✓		
Electricity bill				✓
Money in the bank	✓			
Bank overdraft		✓		
Sales to customers			✓	
Debtors	✓			
Office computers	✓			

Case study activity 3

	Cash Sale	Credit Sale	Cash Purchase	Credit Purchase
Paper bought from a supplier and paid for immediately.			✓	
Products delivered to a customer who will pay at the end of the month.		✓		
Camera components bought from a supplier on credit.				✓
A payment received from a customer for goods purchased online and paid for at the checkout.	✓			

KAPLAN PUBLISHING

Case study activity 4

	£
Sales	156,000
Cost of Sales	-93,600
Wages	-21,060
Administration Expenses	-18,720
Selling Expenses	-12,844
	9,776

Profit / Loss: £ 9,776 Profit

Case study activity 5

	£
Sales	152,880
Cost of Sales	-91,728
Wages	-20,640
Administration Expenses	-18,350
Selling Expenses	-12,590
	9,572

Profit / Loss: £9,572 Profit

An introduction to computerised accounting

2

Introduction

This chapter will give you an insight into the features and benefits of different types of accounting software. It will also look at the advantages of using computerised accounting in comparison to manual bookkeeping.

When choosing which software package would be most suitable for an organisation, the advantages and disadvantages of each should be carefully assessed. This chapter will look at each of these in turn to allow you to make your own assessment in different situations.

When handling data whether it be manual or electronic, it is important to keep it safe and secure. Here, we will look in detail at the many potential threats to data security and the steps that can be taken to safeguard data.

To complete this unit you will need copy of Sage, which is an integrated computerised software package for accounts, or a similar accounting package.

KNOWLEDGE	CONTENTS
Understand the benefits and risks of using accounting software	1 Computerised accounting systems
1.1 Features of accounting software compared to manual bookkeeping	2 Different types of accounting software
1.2 Advantages and disadvantages to users of different types of accounting software	3 The security of accounting data
1.3 Accounting software security	4 Summary and further questions

1 Computerised accounting systems

1.1 Case study: an introduction

📖 Case study

TotalPhoto Ltd has grown considerably since it was established, so Matt Evans and Stuart Lincoln are discussing moving away from a manual bookkeeping system to a computerised accounting package.

Prior to their meeting to discuss this further, Chrissie was asked to research the different features of accounting software and compare it to manual bookkeeping methods in order to identify whether the move would be advantageous for the company. She was also asked to look into the different types of accounting software and outline the advantages and disadvantages of each.

In addition to this, Chrissie researched the potential threats to data security and suggested ways that TotalPhoto could protect their data.

Matt and Stuart will look at the results of Chrissie's findings before making a decision on the best way forward for the company.

Complete the activities as you work through the chapter to ensure a full understanding of its content.

1.2 The use of computerised accounting systems

Manual accounting requires the bookkeeper or accountant to post all transactions manually either into journal ledgers or into spreadsheets via a computer program such as Excel. The reason that this is considered manual is because each transaction has to be entered individually into the accounting records which can be very time-consuming.

For very small organisations, a simple spreadsheet to record monies in and out of the business may be sufficient. However, once a business becomes larger or more complex, it can be more effective and less time-consuming to use a computerised bookkeeping system.

There are many proprietary versions on the market, each of which works in a similar way. However, they will each offer different approaches to data entry, presentation of reports and so on, as well as additional 'extras' such as stock management modules, budgeting and tax planning.

Some systems also allow a company to integrate a computerised payroll function.

1.3   The benefits of computerised accounting systems

The main benefits of using a computerised bookkeeping system in comparison to a manual system are:

- **It enables quicker, more efficient processing of data** – financial transactions can be entered into the accounting system in batches which speeds up the process of data entry. It will perform calculations such as VAT, additions and subtractions automatically which not only improves efficiency but reduces the risk of human error. Batch processing also helps to improve speed and efficiency, further information on batch control is provided in Chapter 3.

- **There is no need for manual processing of data** – computerised bookkeeping systems complete all the double entry automatically. This reduces the risk of errors within the accounting records and helps to ensure that the financial reports produced are more accurate.

- **Fewer mathematical errors** – because the system completes all the double entry and other mathematical functions (e.g. calculation of percentages) there is reduced opportunity for human error.

- **Accounting documents (e.g. invoices, statements etc) can be generated automatically** – within a computerised accounting system, accounting documents can be tailored to meet the needs of the company. They can also incorporate company details, logos etc. and are produced easily with the click of a button. This again helps with efficiency as it allows a company to automate what would be a lengthy process if completed manually.

- **The reporting process** – the range of information that can be easily produced in reports is wide and varied, meaning businesses can report to various internal and external groups (e.g. management, directors, shareholders, banks etc) in an appropriate format. As the calculations within these reports are performed automatically, it means that the information contained within is usually more accurate and reliable.

- **Cost** – hardware and software prices have fallen dramatically over the last thirty years, making a computerised system affordable to all organisations. In addition, the automation of various accounting processes enables individuals to focus their time on other tasks which contributes to the successful operation of an organisation.

- **Data can be imported or exported to and from other programs** – computerised accounting systems allow data to be easily transferred into and out of other programs – e.g. a spreadsheet or word processing package. This allows you to work more flexibly and prevents the risk of duplication within accounting processes.

1.4 The features of computerised accounting systems

Integrated accounting software interlinks multiple functions within the accounting process.

For example, sales, purchases, the bank, the subsidiary ledgers and the general ledger all work with one another to ensure efficiency and accuracy within the accounting records. Double-entry is completed automatically - essentially, a transaction is entered into the system and all affected accounts and ledgers are automatically updated within the program, reducing the risk of error.

> ### 📖 Case study
>
> TotalPhoto Ltd have sold a suite of camera accessories to a national camera club.
>
> As soon as the sale is made and entered onto the system, the inventory levels will automatically decrease. The sale will be recorded in the relevant accounts and the bank account balance will increase to reflect the income received.
>
> If this was completed manually, it would be a long drawn out process and the risk of human error would be quite high as the transaction is being recorded in numerous places.

1.5 Tools and wizards

Tools and wizards can be used for every accounting process, including:

- setting up new customer/supplier records
- creating price lists
- showing opening balances
- maintaining bank accounts
- updating the nominal ledger
- running an audit trail.

Accounting software enables its users to generate a number of business documents, such as sales orders and control stock, print invoices, credit notes and statements. It also allows users to produce history and financial reports for management and analysis. The list of information available is almost endless, as these wizards have been integrated to make accounting easier on a day-to-day basis.

There are also tools available that allow you to check information or data inputted. Other more complicated processes can also be made easier by using the tools function within Sage.

> ### 💡 Example
>
> Management Accounts are essential to the owners/directors of a business as they are the people responsible for making vital business decisions and rely on the information within these accounts.
>
> To access Management Accounts in Sage, click Tools > period end > month end.
>
> This is a simple and reliable way to get the information the decision-makers require.

Using tools and wizards speeds up the accounting process and assures accuracy if the information is inputted into the system correctly. They also leave less room for errors as only one accounting entry is needed for each transaction rather than two (or three) for a manual system. By processing financial information in this way, it promotes client confidence in the accounting company as their records are updated in a timely manner.

All accounting systems have help menus available to users if they are unsure of how to process a transaction or perform a certain function. On the toolbar at the top of the screen, clicking 'Help' will bring up a menu. From here you can either search for key words i.e. 'process a supplier invoice' and this will bring up a list of help sheets which contain guidance on how to complete this task. Alternatively, click through the  different topics within the help menu which will provide necessary information relating to different functions within the program and their use.

The help menus are a really useful tool for those who are new to using accounting software. Some people even use these to produce their own 'process notes' to form part of the training schedule for new staff members. They also help a business by reducing the amount of training needed by individuals in the organisation and as a result this will increase productivity within the department.

1.6 Reporting

Computerised accounting packages automatically pull all relevant ledger entries for the period reports. Manual accounting takes much longer therefore computerised accounting enables reports to be completed much quicker.

Historically, when manual accounts were produced, reporting could take days (sometimes weeks) as all calculations would have to be performed manually and depending on the amount of data required within the report meant that this could be a lengthy process. Nowadays most reports can be produced at the click of a button and the information contained within them is up to date at the point in which the report was produced. This means that information viewed is a lot more reliable and business decisions can be made much more quickly based on the information given.

Reports can be produced which will help the management to instantly monitor and control the business.

📖 Case study

TotalPhoto Ltd's management have identified an issue with unpaid invoices and ask Chrissie how the accounting software could help to address this.

Chrissie suggests the aged debtor's analysis, which will show which customer accounts are overdue, how much they owe and how old the debt is. This helps the credit control department to see which debts need chasing immediately. As a result, this helps with a very important process in accounting, as the business needs income to operate and if the customers are not paying their debts on time, this could lead to cash flow problems.

If the business has cash flow problems, it could not have enough money to pay its suppliers, which could lead to delays in getting products for resale to customers. In this instance, it would not take long for TotalPhoto to start to fail as a business.

Other reports that can be produced include the trial balance, the statement of profit and loss and the statement of financial position.

- **The trial balance** is essentially a list of all accounts within the system and their balances at any one point in time.

  To produce a trial balance with manual accounting, you need to balance off all of the accounts individually and then draw up a list of all of the accounts and enter their balances onto the correct 'debit' or 'credit' side. There is nothing to say that the accounts would be up to date at that point and there wouldn't really be any way of checking.

With computerised accounting, a user simply selects the 'trial balance' from the reports section and prints it off. All of the debits and credits are automatically created and the accounts automatically balanced off. The information contained within the trial balance is in real time, meaning that it is up to date to the point at which you have run the report.

- **The statement of profit and loss** report contains all of the accounts that relate to the income and expenses of the business. Again, using the accounting system, it would be produced in real-time at the point at which the report was produced. Managers would review the information within the profit and loss account to see whether the figures appear to be correct. If something doesn't look quite right, the accounting system allows users to drill into the figures and produce more detailed analysis on the income and expenses by running the analysis reports for the required accounts. This means that the reporting process within Sage not only increases productivity but it also reduces the stress levels of staff and enables them to work more efficiently.

We will cover reports in more detail in relation to Sage Line 50 later on in this book. You will also practice producing a number of different reports and you will see numerous formats and layouts available for each. It really depends on the needs of the business as to which report is the most suitable for each particular task.

Templates for financial reports are available to meet the needs of individual organisations where logos and business-related information can be included. All businesses have many clients and users of financial reporting, it would therefore not be cost-effective or possible to design individual report layouts for every client/user of the software.

Whilst there are many reports available with different options for layouts and the information contained within, it would be impossible to be able to meet the needs of every individual user.

1.7 Importing and exporting data

🔍 Definitions

Importing data means taking information such as a file from one location on a computer to another location on a computer so that you can work with or use that file/information in a different format.

Exporting data is the same in reverse – sending data from one location in your computer to another location, either internally or externally.

Information that can be imported or exported can come in many formats which include files produced by other programs such as spreadsheets, word processors or other accounting packages.

In accounting, this is a really useful tool as not all organisations will use accounting software for their day-to-day operations.

🔆 Example

A company may use a database to store all customer/supplier information. This information can be imported into the accounting software package to save inputting it twice.

In terms of the information that can be imported, this includes:

- customers information
- supplier information
- stock information
- asset data.

Financial transactions computed in one type of software cannot be imported into another type of software. Accounting transactions need to be produced at source within the accounting software.

The most common tool used in accounting is exporting data from the accounting software into spreadsheet format using a program such as Excel.

Reports produced within the accounting software can be exported to spreadsheet format and then the data can be manipulated to suit the needs of the business.

For example, a company might produce an aged debtor's report and export this into Excel. From here they can then add or remove information as required and then produce charts and graphs to make the information easier to see at a glance. They may do this month on month so that they can spot any trends in the data which will enable them to take appropriate action within the credit control department.

Many organisations will use the import/export function in their day-to-day operations as sometimes the accounting package that they are using is limited in terms of the information that can be produced and how it can be manipulated. Importing and exporting data not only saves time processing large volumes of information, but it allows an organisation to work more flexibly with the information given. It also reduces the risk of human error as the same information isn't being manually inputted to a number of different places.

Test your understanding 1

What are the benefits of being able to import and export data to and from other programs?

Tick all that apply.

	✓
It saves time	
It reduces the risk of human error	
To be able to communicate information in different formats	
It ensures all data is backed up	
It enables all accounting transactions to be modified	
To be able to work with data more flexibly	

Test your understanding 2

If you are unsure how to complete a task, what do you click on?

Put a tick in the correct box.

	✓
Help menu	
Tools menu	
File menu	
Task menu	

Test your understanding 3

Consider the following statement:

An advantage of producing reports using accounting software is that it shows real-time financial information

Put a tick in the correct box to show if the statement is true or false.

	✓
True	
False	

2 Different types of accounting software

2.1 'Off the shelf' accounting software

Many accounting software packages can be bought 'off the shelf', from retail outlets or suppliers. They typically come in a box with a CD to load the software onto a computer and a user manual to help with set up and instructions of how to process financial transactions.

You may have come across some of these in your day-to-day work but examples include: Sage (there are many versions of this), Quickbooks and CCH. You will find that these are available to purchase from retail outlets specialising in computer or office goods or online via their websites. 'Off the shelf' accounting packages are easy to install and usually have a step by step wizard to help you set up your accounting platform.

The main advantage of 'off the shelf' accounting software is the cost. It works out cheaper than some other software types as effectively you purchase a license for a certain number of users at a fixed fee. This cost is then spread out across multiple users and once purchased, there are no further costs unless you wish to upgrade the software to a later version.

For a small business, they may decide that the current version of the software is sufficient for their day-to-day operations and therefore they may decide not to upgrade. If they do upgrade, they will only pay for the upgrade and, again, this is a fixed, one-off amount. With 'off the shelf' software, there are external training courses and webinars available which takes the ownership away from the employer. Many suppliers of 'off the shelf' software also have helpdesks that users of the system can contact if they are experiencing problems; members of their specialist teams will assist, rather than problems having to be dealt with internally.

'Off the shelf' software can be complicated to use (especially for small businesses) and may contain sections that are not needed. It tries to offer something for every kind of company and therefore is not specific to one particular industry. This may mean a shortfall for specialist businesses, which could be a disadvantage. If this is the case, companies may have to alter the way they operate to fit in with the software's limitations, possibly resulting in further training for staff and new processes. It can also take some time for new users to learn how to use the software properly which could slow down the production of financial information in the early stages of use. However, in comparison to manual accounting, an 'off the shelf' accounting package will dramatically increase speed and productivity within an accounts department and reduce the risk of human error.

2.2   Bespoke accounting software

Bespoke accounting software is designed and written to meet the individual needs of an organisation. When choosing this option for accounting, a business will look at all aspects of their day-to-day operations and decide what it is that they want the system to do for them, and what information they would like the system to produce.

Software developers will then be brought in to design and implement the system; this could be done in house (for larger organisations) or by an external company who specialise in doing this. If taking the latter option, it is important that the company has access to the source code for the software. If they do not have the source code for the software, there is a danger that the business can be exposed.

The main disadvantage of using bespoke accounting software is that it takes time to develop, implement and test the software before it can be used. If it does not work how the company desire, it will take additional time to go back and amend it. All of this comes at a cost and it can become expensive in relation to 'off the shelf' software packages.

Another disadvantage is that all staff will need specialised training on how to use the software. This will have to be done internally which again comes at a cost. Overall, using bespoke software proves a very expensive although sophisticated option, especially for large specialist businesses.

There are many advantages of bespoke accounting software. As it is made to work how the company likes to work and to fit their business needs, it means that if a company changes the way it works, the software can be changed to meet this demand.

The software is continuously developed and updated, so it should never become outdated which can prove to be a massive benefit to the company. As the software is generated internally, this means that there are no licensing costs or annual fees in comparison to 'off the shelf' accounting software. If users of the system are experiencing problems, these can be solved in house rather than having to contact an external help desk which means less supervision should be needed.

Bespoke software could also potentially offer a company a competitive advantage because you can design specialist features that may not be used/available to your competitors.

2.3 Cloud-based accounting software

> **Q Definition**
>
> **Cloud computing** refers to the delivery of various computing services online via web-based applications, using a network of servers connected to the internet rather than a direct connection to local servers or in-house networks.
>
> Cloud computing allows files to be stored and managed remotely, meaning that data can be downloaded from any location. The remote nature of the storage also means that important information is backed up safely, regardless of issues with your computer or network.
>
> Therefore, cloud-based accounting software allows tasks to be completed online and for data to be safely stored remotely.

Cloud-based accounting software is a relatively new way of accounting, which enables all accountancy tasks to be completed online, 'in the cloud'. Storing information remotely, in the cloud, increases the safety of stored information where the chances of unauthorised access from external sources are virtually nil. As the data is stored virtually and off the premises, this also protects it from natural disasters such as floods and fires.

Most common applications have evolved and are now offering this service such as SageOne, Xero, Quickbooks Kashflow and Clearbooks. Many companies that have moved towards a cloud-based version of accounting feel that it has revolutionised the way in which they work.

The software is available to authorised users anywhere, on any device that has an internet connection. This means that the user does not necessarily have to be in the office in order to access the software and complete their duties. Users can even download applications onto their smart phones and complete their day-to-day accounting transactions whilst on the move. Consequently, accounting is more flexible and urgent tasks can easily be completed on an ad hoc basis.

From a management perspective this is also a more productive new way of working. Managers may not necessarily be available in the office all of the time. Cloud-based accounting means that they are not restricted to viewing activity and productivity on the company premises. This enables a smooth flow of work and action to be taken much more quickly if productivity slows or work is not being completed in the correct manner.

> ### 📖 Case study
>
> One of TotalPhoto Ltd's customers is chasing a credit note, which was due three weeks ago.
>
> As TotalPhoto only have a desktop version of accounting software, it will be necessary to wait for a member of the accounts team to process the credit note in the office. No one is available to do this, so the customer does not receive the credit note despite their complaint.
>
> However, if they were using cloud accounting, the user in the accounts department could view the customer account via the internet or via their smartphone application and gather the required information, create the credit note and send it straightaway.
>
> Therefore, not only does this increase productivity, but it presents a good impression of the company and creates solid relationships with customers.

Cloud-based accounting is a cost-effective way of working because the company computer costs are reduced. Companies pay a monthly subscription for access to the software for a specific number of users. This means that there is no limit to the number of users who are able to access the program and different levels of access can be set which helps to protect company data.

Another advantage of cloud-based accounting is that all software maintenance, version upgrades, system administration costs and server failures are managed by the cloud accounting service provider. In terms of cash flow for a company, this is excellent as the management know exactly how much they are paying and with this being paid monthly, there are no unexpected costs or additional upgrade fees. However, it may not be cost effective for a small company to keep paying subscription fees compared to purchasing 'off the shelf' software. A small company may only have a handful of users so having to pay a monthly subscription to be able to use the software may work out more expensive than if they purchased an 'off the shelf' package.

Another disadvantage to cloud based accounting is that companies have no direct control over their information. The server which is supplied and controlled by the software provider could be anywhere outside the UK. Different countries have different rules and this could mean that a government in another country could be looking at your remotely stored files.

In addition to this, updates may be a problem. The software provider will decide what additional features they are going to add to the program and when this will happen. This means that users can only have what the accounting provider offers and can only update processes when the general software update occurs. Ultimately this does not allow much flexibility in terms of being able to easily change the way companies work to reflect the ever changing demands of their business.

There can be problems when backing up data, as most cloud accounting software providers do not have the ability for a company to take a backup of its data and export it or save it to their own computer system. Therefore the company can be limited to printing out selected reports. This means that changing to another package or just keeping a long-term record without having to keep paying the monthly subscription can cause significant issues.

2.4 Choosing the correct software: 'off the shelf' vs bespoke

When comparing 'off the shelf' software with bespoke software, the following should be considered before choosing which is the right option for an organisation:

Cost

- 'Off the shelf' software involves the purchase price of the product. There is then usually an annual license fee to pay; companies have to pay a fee per user of the software.

- Bespoke software is extremely expensive at the outset. It is impossible to give a price as it is dependent on the size and complexity of the software build that the company needs. It will always cost many thousands of pounds however as you own the software, there are no license fees.

Levels of support for users

- 'Off the shelf' software has so many users that there is a wealth of online community support. Many software programs provide online 'web chat', e-mail and telephone support facilities. Some software providers charge for maintenance and support functions.

- In relation to bespoke software, there are no means of direct self-help support or online communities, however, as there is direct access to the developer who will provide support, this means that this is not necessary.

Timeframe for development

- 'Off the shelf' software has already been developed and therefore once you have purchased the package, the software is loaded onto a computer and is instantly available to start using. The only problem that some users may encounter at this point is whether or not they know how to use the software.

- Bespoke software takes months to develop and the more complex software builds can take as long as a year, dependent on how many developers are working on it. Once developed, the software then needs to be tested and any problems detected and amended before any data can be transferred into it. The added problem of transferring old data from another program into the new one will probably follow, although some of the information may be exported from an old program depending on how the new bespoke version has been designed. This means that the initial setup could take some time and all of the information from the old system must be checked for accuracy to ensure the integrity of the data.

Range of functions used by the business

- 'Off the shelf' software has so many functions available that most companies will not need all of them and therefore there will be some functions that they will never use at all. The software is designed under a 'one size fits all' basis in an attempt to suit all business needs, so what functions one company uses another may not.

- Bespoke software only has functions that an individual company has specified that they need. These should be designed and implemented to fit in with the company's processes to ensure smooth automation and increased productivity where possible.

Frequency and ease of updates

- Updates are available with 'off the shelf' software, it depends on the software provider used as to whether there is a fee for this service. The software updates will be decided upon by the software provider and will not necessarily match the demands of an individual business. In addition to this, updates are installed as and when the software provider decide, not necessarily in a timeframe to suit a particular business' needs.

- Updates are free with bespoke software and will be agreed with the program designers. If a particular function within the program needs to be added or amended due to company expansion for example, then this will be done in a timeframe that suits the business needs. The program developers if working with an external company will charge for this service.

Level of training required to use the software

- When introduced, 'off the shelf' software usually comes with training needs for an organisation's staff. Employees need to learn how to navigate the software to meet the needs of the organisation. Each user will have different tasks to complete using the program. This means that depending on the user, there may be quite a lot of new ways of working to learn. This can increase cost and slow down productivity. The software provider will provide external training courses as well as webinars/online videos for them to use to help them get to grips with how the system works.

- Bespoke software needs very little training, as it is built to function in the same way as the company works. If a whole new system is built and all users are new to it, staff could get involved in the testing phase to get them used to using it. All training would be conducted in house with the developers or senior staff members who have been involved in the changeover.

Type of subscription

- 'Off the shelf' subscriptions vary by software provider and can include some or all of the following charges: upgrades, software support, monthly or annual licensing fees, per user fee, per-website or installation licenses.

- There are no subscription fees with bespoke software because the company owns the software.

📝 Test your understanding 4

Match the following features to the relevant software by ticking the correct one.

	Bespoke Software	'Off the Shelf' Software
Already developed		
Tailored to company specification		
Instant installation		
Takes time to develop and install		
Requires a subscription		
No subscription needed		

2.5   Choosing the correct software: traditional vs cloud

Cost

- Traditional accounting software can be costly, as well as set up costs there are costs involved in system upgrades. In addition to this, customer support can be expensive.

- With cloud software there are no upfront fees for hardware packages such as servers - instead smaller fixed monthly fees are paid. The only downside to this is that it does involve committing to a contract. With there being no way of backing up data to the organisation's computer hardware, it also makes transferring from a cloud-based version back to traditional software more difficult.

Levels of support for users

- With traditional accounting software, support is usually made available via telephone during office hours. This can end up being quite costly, time consuming and is not always convenient for those who work longer hours or whose working hours are outside of the traditional 9 – 5 Monday to Friday.

- Cloud-based software users usually feel much more supported because support is available online 24/7. This is much more flexible for those who work unsociable hours, or for those who might want to complete their business' bookkeeping duties in the evening.

Range of functions used by the business

- Often traditional accounting software will only work across one platform. The functions available using traditional software are also restricted to whatever is built in to the program they are using.

- All accounting functions can be accessed via the cloud. A range of functions are available and these are regularly reviewed and updated free of charge by the software provider. Different levels of access to different functions can be set for the varying levels of job roles within the organisation.

Frequency and ease of updates

- Traditional accounting updates can be expensive and the user has to remember to do them. In order to run the updates, there must be sufficient space on the server and this can sometimes take considerable time to complete. The updates with traditional software are not always as up to date as other types of software and are not always easy to accomplish.

- Cloud-based accounting updates are automatically processed by the server. Notifications of updates are communicated to the user by the software provider so that the company can utilise the software properly as the technology evolves. The cost of upgrades is included in the monthly subscription and therefore no additional costs are incurred.

Upgrade capacity

- With traditional accounting, upgrades are not always possible due to the storage capacity of the computer system. This then involves the costly task of having to expand the system memory in order to install the upgrade.

- With cloud-based accounting, there is no danger of running out of space to upgrade as this is managed by the service provider. The cost of your monthly fee however, is dependent on the size of your storage package.

Level of training required to use the software

- There are many different training options available with both traditional software and cloud-based accounting, these include:

    - external training by the software provider

    - courses run by an accredited training company

    - online webinars and training videos

    - user manuals.

Access from multiple devices

- Traditional accounting is restricted to working on one computer, if the user wanted to take information away from the office to work with elsewhere it would mean saving their work to a device such as a USB stick. This poses a security risk as sensitive information could be lost in transportation.

- With cloud-based accounting, users can access and work with their software on multiple devices from anywhere with an internet connection - for example, on laptops, ipads/tablets and mobile telephones.

Type of subscription

- Traditional accounting subscriptions can include a one-off fee with the potential for additional costs for upgrades etc. If licenses are put in place, they are done so on a per user basis.

- Cloud-based accounting requires a contract commitment with the service provider and a monthly subscription fee.

Access to the internet

- Traditional accounting does not require an internet connection.
- An authorised user can access cloud-based software anywhere in the world where there is an internet connection.

✎ Test your understanding 5

Alba works in the accounts department at NB Solutions Ltd. She has received an e-mail to say that she may have overlooked something within the company accounts but is on holiday abroad. It cannot wait until she returns home.

Which software would allow Alba to access the information?

Put a tick in the correct box.

	✓
'Off the shelf'	
Bespoke	
Cloud-based	

✎ Test your understanding 6

Different types of software have different advantages.

Match the relevant software to its statement.

	Cloud	Bespoke	'Off the Shelf'
You can access it anywhere in the world with an internet connection			
Is developed to meet the individual company needs			
Can be changed to meet the changing demands of a company			
Can be used on any device (laptop, tablet, smartphone)			
Loads instantly onto a computer			
Has a widespread self-help community forum			
Has online support 24/7			

3 The security of accounting data

3.1 Threats to data security

All businesses, regardless of what they do or how they operate, handle confidential information on a daily basis.

The information is a necessary commodity and is extremely valuable to the successful operation of an organisation.

Company information and sensitive information about other organisations and individuals should always be kept safe and secure, not only to protect the reputation of the business, but to protect itself from competitors within the market.

All information they store within their systems and processes is protected by law under The Data Protection Act.

3.2 Commercial information

The data held by the accounts department will include company information such as:

- sales data
- product or service specifications
- customer and supplier details.

This information may be commercially sensitive. For example, the price paid for a particular product, or discounts given to customers. If a competitor of the business knew this information they might be able to use it as a competitive advantage. It is therefore imperative to protect customer information.

3.3 Personal information

An organisation will also hold personal information. Personal information held about individuals, such as employees and customers, is protected by law. The Data Protection Act sets out rules about how personal data can be used. The Act sets out eight data protection principles which must be followed when processing personal data.

The information must be:

1. used fairly and lawfully
2. used for limited, specifically stated purposes
3. used in a way that is adequate, relevant and not excessive
4. accurate

5.　kept for no longer than is absolutely necessary

6.　handled according to people's data protection rights

7.　kept safe and secure

8.　not transferred outside the European Economic Area without adequate protection

Any organisations who process personal data must register with the Information Commissioner's Office in order to be permitted to process data. The Information Commissioner's Office (ICO) is the UK's independent body set up to uphold information rights. You can find out how personal information is protected by visiting their website: https://www.ico.org.uk

Whether personal and sensitive information is held on computer or in a paper based filing system, it must be kept safe and secure. This means it must be kept away from any unauthorised access. It would be wrong to leave personal data open to be viewed by just anyone.

Test your understanding 7

Tick the appropriate box for the statements provided:

Commercial information is information that can be sold to anyone, so it does not have to be kept confidential.

True ☐ or False ☐

You have finished working on a document, you have made notes on paper that you do not need anymore. Are you going to:

Discard the paper in the bin ☐　　　Shred the paper ☐

3.4　Viruses

For the above reasons, it is vital that all information in the possession of an organisation is kept secure and private. One of the most feared threats to this are computer viruses.

The best way to understand the concept of a computer virus is to think about a human being having the flu virus. Let's call them the 'host.' When they come into contact with another human they infect them with the virus.

The virus can just keep on replicating itself and spreading from human to human until there is an epidemic. In the same way, a computer virus needs a 'host' cell such as a program, file or document. When that is sent to another computer that too becomes infected.

These viruses are cleverly hidden and can be unwittingly sent from user to user. People often do not realise that they have an infected computer until they experience problems with using their programs. The more severe viruses have been known to spread to millions of users and have damaged their systems, or in some cases have destroyed them completely.

Unfortunately, viruses are created by people who write bad codes intended to change the way in which a computer operates. There have been instances where people experimenting have accidently sent out bad codes, however it is usually an intentional action by someone who known as a **cybercriminal**. They send the bad code out and it will attach itself to a program or file on the recipient user's computer. The virus may not do any damage immediately and will usually only become active when the individual runs the file that it has attached itself to (until then, it is effectively sleeping). Once the user runs that program the bad code becomes active and the computer is infected. At this point, it can in turn infect other computers on the same network.

A virus attack can completely destroy accounting data and files, resulting in the loss of client and business information. A severe attack can destroy an accounting system completely making it unusable. An attack can also create openings for unauthorised users known as hackers to view and steal sensitive information and data. The nature of accounting often means sending customers information electronically and therefore viruses can be inadvertently sent to the client.

The first line of defence against a virus is to backup data and save it in a safe place such as a locked fire proof cabinet. It is good practice to have a further backed up copy stored in outside premises in case something happens to the file that is kept in the office. If storing data in the cloud, backups should be regularly updated to capture new data, the computer is set to automatically do a backup and as the information stored is real-time information, the most up to date data is always available to access.

To protect data from viruses, anti-virus software should be installed on the system and regularly updated. Anti-virus software is installed onto the computer system to scan information such as e-mails for viruses and will block any content that appears suspect. Viruses can be extremely dangerous as they can shut down a whole system in a very short space of time. If data becomes corrupt, you will not be able to see or use it therefore it is very important that an organisation protects itself with anti-virus software.

Individuals should always close their computer screen if leaving their workstation and lock the screen to avoid unauthorised people from viewing information or accessing the computer.

Test your understanding 8

Viruses can.....

Tick all of the options below that complete the sentence correctly.

	✓
Cause loss of information	
Can be easily fixed	
Cause the system to crash	
Infect all computers on the same network	
Only be harmful for s short period of time	
Cause a loss in productivity	

3.5 Hacking

Just like a burglar enters premises without permission, hackers gain access to people's computers without permission. Once they have done so, the hackers can do anything from stealing information to having control of the computer. Sophisticated hackers can see everything that the user is doing.

Hackers can gain access to computers in several ways such as through viruses, insecure wireless connections, e-mails, fake internet sites and social media. Hackers are constantly looking for weaknesses in computer programs and, just like a burglar will take advantage of an open window and sneak in, a hacker will do the same with a vulnerable computer.

If a hacker manages to access accounting data they can cause irreparable damage to the business. They can access all the clients' information and use it to commit identity theft, steal passwords and change or delete data.

These kind of attacks can cause huge financial losses to an organisation. The firm would have to inform all its clients that this had happened, resulting in damage to the reputation of the company and potentially the loss of clients.

To protect accounting data from hackers, effective use of passwords by employees is key. It is important to keep passwords safe and secure and change them regularly in line with the company procedures or immediately suspecting that someone has found out what the password is.

An organisation with a number of employees will usually have a system that prompts the user to change their password when it is time to do so. In addition, you should not use the same password for different programs, this way if a hacker guesses one password they do not have access to everything.

The harder it is for someone to guess your password, the harder it is for them to access sensitive information. You should avoid the use of names or dates that are personal to you as quite often these can be easy to guess. Ideally a password should contain both upper and lower case letters, numbers and symbols. Individuals should NEVER share your password with anyone and should always close your computer screen when you leave your workstation and lock the screen to avoid unauthorised people from viewing information or using your computer.

Encrypting data is effective against hackers. This is where your information is scrambled up so that it looks like nonsense. Only people who have access to the key stored on your hardware can unscramble it. So, a hacker may still manage to break in to the computer but they would not be able to understand the information.

Another way of protecting an organisation from hackers is to only keep the data that is of use. Client/customer information such as credit card numbers, dates of birth or other personal or sensitive data may be of no use, but is tempting for hackers. Therefore employees must be vigilant and remove the information.

Ensuring that a good security software package is in place and keeping it updated is another way in which data can be kept secure.

📝 Test your understanding 9

You have recently set up online banking for your current account.

You need to set a password for access to the online banking facilities. Which of the following would make a good password? Tick the TWO best answers from the options given.

	✓
Something you cannot remember	
Something other people are not likely to know	
Something obvious	
The word 'password'	
Your name and year of birth	
A combination of letters, numbers and symbols	
Something you saved on your PC in a file called Passwords	

Test your understanding 10

You have a colleague who is also a good friend. They have forgotten their password to the system and need to quickly amend some figures before their meeting.

They have asked to use your password temporarily, what do you do?

Put a tick in the correct box.

	✓
Give them your password but tell them not to tell anyone else what it is	
Give them your password for now and then change it when they have gone into their meeting	
Refuse to give them your password	
Log in for them so they don't know what your password is	

Test your understanding 11

Below is a list of statements. State which are true and which are false.

Statement	True/False
Passwords can be shared with colleagues who are doing the same type work.	
All cabinet drawers with personal or commercial information in should be kept locked.	
If leaving your work station, you must ensure that the screen is blank and computer access blocked.	

3.6 Phishing

Phishing is an attempt to trick people into revealing sensitive information such as passwords, bank details or any other kind of sensitive financial information. The ultimate goal is financial theft. There are also phishing attacks where they not only try to steal information but also attach a virus to your system.

Phishing usually occurs in the form of an e-mail that looks like it came from a genuine organisation, for example a bank. A common trick is to tell the recipient that there has been some unusual activity on their account.

They must sign into the account using the link provided (fake web address that looks like the banks) and verify their details in order to be able to continue using their account. It will say that an immediate response is required or your account will be suspended or closed.

Anyone clicking the link and providing the information has just given a thief all they need to steal from their bank account. People often receive these kinds of e-mails from organisations that they don't even have an account with. Companies may receive an e-mail that appears to be from one of their genuine clients. They are designed to trick the user into giving out financial information about the company or may activate a virus once opened.

Example

A recent phishing scheme e-mail reported in the USA targeted accounting firm employees. It looked like it was from a genuine client and asked the employee to open an attachment.

When opened, key-logging malware was launched that could see every keystroke the employee made.

It even got past encrypted data because the keystrokes were recorded by the malware before they were encrypted.

Phishing can cause a major threat to accounting data because sensitive data about clients and their customers can be used to gain access to their bank accounts or be used for other fraudulent financial transactions. Information about a company can be divulged to competitors or in some cases sold for the purpose of causing financial ruin.

If users wish to protect your data from phishing, they need to remember that no reputable organisation will EVER contact them and ask for a password. If the sender of an e-mail is not known, e-mails should not be opened and a virus scan should be performed.

If you are unsure of an e-mail because you know the sender, contact them to ask if they have sent you the e-mail. Hover over any strange looking links with your cursor to see if it is spelled correctly or is an unusual address. You should delete any obvious suspicious e-mail unopened and if you are unsure, you should report any strange activity to the I.T department.

Test your understanding 12

You receive an email from a client asking you to click on a link. It is unusual for them to contact you via email, what do you do?

There are TWO correct answers. Put a tick in the relevant boxes.

	✓
Ignore the email	
Hover over the address and if it looks genuine, click on the link	
Forward it to your supervisor	
Click on the link	
Contact the client to ask if they have sent the email	

3.7 System crashes

If a system crashes, it means that the system stops working properly and shuts itself down. This happens because data or other files can suddenly develop errors that the system cannot handle or recognise. These corrupt files are commonly known as computer bugs.

Power failures and problems with other programs or networks can also cause a system to crash. If this happens, there is a chance that all data files could be lost and therefore it is essential to protect data by taking regular backups. If a system has to be restored using a backup from before the crash happened, any transactions completed since would need to be re-entered. However, if data is stored in the cloud, it is automatically backed up on a regular basis. This means that when the system is backup and running, the number of transactions that need to be re-entered is minimal.

3.8 Employee fraud in accounting

Employee fraud is where an employee steals money from a business by altering or creating accounting records, in order to make missing money that they have stolen, look like legitimate transactions.

There are many ways in which this can happen, as shown in the examples on the following page.

> ### :'Q'·: Example
>
> **Accounts payable fraud** – an employee sets up a fake supplier and charges the company for goods or services that have not actually been provided.
>
> **Personal purchases** – an employee uses company funds to pay for personal purchases and records the payments as legitimate business expenses in the accounting system.
>
> **Payroll fraud** – an employee processing payroll transactions sets up ghost employees on the system and pays them, intercepting the money for themselves.

Not only do these instances of fraud cause financial losses for the business, but often the employee is altering data either by deleting, adding or changing figures. This affects the integrity of the accounting data which is used to produce the year-end financial statements and to calculate their taxes. Incorrect information can lead to penalties and fines. There is also a risk of the system crashing or the employee causing a bad code to be generated and introduce a virus.

To protect accounting data from employee fraud, the company should introduce segregation of duties across the department/accounting process. Segregation of duties is where more than one employee is responsible for every stage of an accounting process. By having work checked more than once, this reduces the risk of employee fraud occurring and the temptation to attempt it.

> ### :'Q'·: Examples
>
> The cashier taking cash to the bank on behalf of a business should not be the same person who writes out the paying in slip to the bank. This reduces the danger of cash disappearing into the cashier's pocket.
>
> There should also be a supervisor/line manager overseeing accounting activities on a regular basis. This involves checking things such as data entries onto computers, payments etc. with specified limits on payments over a certain amount e.g. payments over £2,500 need to be authorised by a senior member of staff.
>
> Employees should also be encouraged to report suspicious activity.

3.9 Corrupt files

Corrupt files are files that suddenly stop working. There are several reasons for this happening.

A common reason is that the file has developed a bad sector - this is something that can happen randomly and unfortunately little can prevent it. Sometimes there is a fault or bug that may cause a file not to work properly, but it starts working again. The problem may never recur but the system needs checking by the I.T department to ensure nothing more serious is happening behind the scenes.

The more serious way of files becoming corrupt is if a bug occurs due to the system having a virus. This poses a threat to accounting data as it can result in the loss of some or all accounting data. To protect against this, regular backups of data should be taken. Storing data in a cloud will ensure that the most up to date information is always available. Frequent virus checks will also help protect files from becoming corrupt.

3.10 Natural disasters and accidental deletion

Unexpected events occur in all over the world and are classed as natural disasters. These include fires, floods and earthquakes. Data is always vulnerable in the case of one of these events.

Accidental deletion is when someone removes a file or other data that should not have been removed from the system. This is usually by mistake or because of human error. Accidental deletion can happen by clicking on the wrong key or sequence of keys on the computer or by trying to correct an entry by deleting it incorrectly. Sometimes people try to speed up some of their working practices by copying and pasting information but sometimes this can lead to accidental data loss.

Accidental deletion or natural disasters could result in the loss of all accounting data files which causes major setbacks for a business. If client information is lost, this could cause major problems for the company and will lead to financial loss as well as having a negative effect on their reputation.

In order to protect accounting data, backup data should be stored in a fireproof cabinet high off the floor. Backups should be taken on a regular basis, and at least once a day in most businesses. In addition, individual files should regularly be backed up whilst working on them. There is little more frustrating than spending an hour producing a document or a spreadsheet only to lose it and not to have a backup.

Copies of backups should be kept securely to prevent unauthorised access or accidental damage. It is good practice to keep a backup at a secondary location (i.e. off the premises). This way, if there is a fire or a burglary the backup data will not be destroyed or stolen. Some businesses may still take physical backups off site (such as a CD), but this increases the risk of that backup being lost or stolen while away from the office. It is becoming increasingly common for organisations to pay an IT company to keep remote backups electronically.

Storing data in cloud is also another secure method as it is always accessible from anywhere with an internet connection.

3.11 Risks of using a computerised system

Computerised accounting systems may offer a lot of advantages to businesses, but organisations must also be aware of the potential risks posed by such systems. These risks have been shown above, and can be categorised as:

- **Physical risks** – caused by system failure, theft, damage or loss or corruption of data, and access to systems or data by unauthorised users.

- **Virus threats** – the risk of a computer virus (or similar) being introduced to a network, with the resultant loss of or damage to data.

- **Legal threats** – from contravention of legislation such as the Data Protection Act (1998) by an organisation in the way that it stores or uses personal data.

Accounting data is particularly at risk, because it is highly confidential and potentially highly valuable to other people.

Test your understanding 13

You have been working on a confidential document on your computer and have to leave the office for ten minutes to deal with a customer.

How can you keep the information on your screen confidential?

	✓
Switch the computer off	
Use the screen lock facility to lock the computer screen	
Stay at your desk	
Put some papers over the screen to hide the information	

Test your understanding 14

Complete the following sentences:

a) I need to go to the bathroom, I should use my computer _____ lock.

b) _____ software is another way of keeping information safe and secure.

c) Backed up computer data should be stored in _____ cabinets.

---

4 Summary and further questions

In this chapter we have considered why organisations use computerised accounting systems and the different types of software available, including 'off the shelf' packages, bespoke products and cloud-based applications. You should have a good understanding of the advantages and disadvantages of all of these types of software and which are most appropriate for different organisations.

We have also looked in depth at security software and the risks and threats presented by computerised accounting.

Let us return to our case study to see how Chrissie applies this knowledge.

Case study activity 6

Chrissie is called into a meeting with Matt and Stuart to discuss the move to a computerised accounting system for TotalPhoto Ltd. She is asked to state the benefits of using accounting software compared to the existing manual accounting system.

Which of the following are advantages of using accounting software? Tick all correct answers.

	✓
Money can be saved as no accounting staff are required	
All accounting software packages offer online chat support	
Data can be processed more efficiently and accurately	
Invoices and statements can be generated automatically	
It removes the threat of viruses	
It reduces the likelihood of mathematical errors	
Data can easily be exported to other programs	
The Data Protection Act is no longer a consideration	

📖✏ Case study activity 7

Having decided that an accounting software system is required and decided that TotalPhoto Ltd is too small to need a bespoke package, Matt and Stuart are unsure of whether to buy an 'off the shelf' product or a cloud-based accounting solution.

They ask Chrissie for her advice on the matter. Which TWO of the following statements would be correct advice for her to offer?

	✓
With cloud-based accounting software, it is not necessary to be in the office as applications can be accessed anywhere on any device, as long as there is an internet connection. This means greater flexibility and easier access to data.	
Updates are not as easy and are more expensive with cloud-based accounting systems. Furthermore, the user needs to remember to run the updates, unlike 'off the shelf' packages where updates are automatic and quicker.	
'Off the shelf' accounting software often comes with much better support – this is available 24 hours a day, 7 days a week, via online chat communities and therefore is better suited for those working long hours.	
Traditional accounting software can prove more expensive, as there are both set up costs and the additional upgrade costs. Cloud-based software is usually paid for by a monthly subscription, so although there is a contract, the fee is fixed.	
All accounting functions can be accessed via the cloud and therefore it is easier for everyone to access the data, including customers and individuals with no connection to the company. Everyone has the same level of access, which is fairer.	

📖✏ Case study activity 8

Chrissie has been asked to create her own unique password for the accounting system. Which of the following passwords should she use?

a) Password123

b) CNorris011200

c) ChrissieTotalPhoto

d) 4yXkj2fR!*

📖✎ **Case study activity 9**

Chrissie is aware that there are a number of risks when using computerised accounting systems and IT to support the accounting function.

Match the relevant threat from the picklist below to its statement.

Statement	Threat
Enters your computer from infected files or programs	
Enters your computer through emails	
Can trace every stroke of a key you make on your computer	

Picklist

Hacking

Phishing

Viruses

Answers to chapter activities

Test your understanding 1

	✔
It saves time	✔
It reduces the risk of human error	✔
To be able to communicate information in different formats	✔
It ensures all data is backed up	
It enables all accounting transactions to be modified	
To be able to work with data more flexibly	✔

Test your understanding 2

	✔
Help menu	✔
Tools menu	
File menu	
Task menu	

Test your understanding 3

An advantage of producing reports using accounting software is that it shows real-time financial information

	✔
True	✔
False	

KAPLAN PUBLISHING

Test your understanding 4

	Bespoke Software	'Off the Shelf' Software
Already developed		✓
Tailored to company specification	✓	
Instant installation		✓
Takes time to develop and install	✓	
Requires a subscription		✓
No subscription needed	✓	

Test your understanding 5

	✓
'Off the shelf'	
Bespoke	
Cloud-based	✓

Test your understanding 6

	Cloud	Bespoke	'Off the Shelf'
You can access it anywhere in the world with an internet connection	✓		
Is developed to meet the individual company needs		✓	
Can be changed to meet the changing demands of a company		✓	
Can be used on any device (laptop, tablet, smartphone)	✓		
Loads instantly onto a computer			✓
Has a widespread self-help community forum			✓
Has online support 24/7	✓		

✎ Test your understanding 7

Commercial information is information that can be sold to anyone, so it does not have to be kept confidential.

True ☐ or False ☑

You have finished working on a document, you have made notes on paper that you do not need anymore. Are you going to:

Discard the paper in the bin ☐   Shred the paper ☑

✎ Test your understanding 8

	✓
Cause loss of information	✓
Can be easily fixed	
Cause the system to crash	✓
Infect all computers on the same network	✓
Only be harmful for s short period of time	
Cause a loss in productivity	✓

✎ Test your understanding 9

	✓
Something you cannot remember	
Something other people are not likely to know	✓
Something obvious	
The word 'password'	
Your name and year of birth	
A combination of letters, numbers and symbols	✓
Something you saved on your PC in a file called Passwords	

Test your understanding 10

	✓
Give them your password but tell them not to tell anyone else what it is	
Give them your password for now and then change it when they have gone into their meeting	
Refuse to give them your password	✓
Log in for them so they don't know what your password is	

Test your understanding 11

Statement	True/False
Passwords can be shared with colleagues who are doing the same type work.	False
All cabinet drawers with personal or commercial information in should be kept locked.	True
If leaving your work station, you must ensure that the screen is blank and computer access blocked.	True

Test your understanding 12

	✓
Ignore the email	
Hover over the address and if it looks genuine, click on the link	✓
Forward it to your supervisor	
Click on the link	
Contact the client to ask if they have sent the email	✓

✎ Test your understanding 13

	✓
Switch the computer off	
Use the screen lock facility to lock the computer screen	✓
Stay at your desk	
Put some papers over the screen to hide the information	

✎ Test your understanding 14

a) I need to go to the bathroom, I should use my computer **screen** lock.

b) **Anti-virus** software is another way of keeping information safe and secure.

c) Backed up computer data should be stored in **fireproof** cabinets.

📖✏ Case study activity 6

	✓
Money can be saved as no accounting staff are required	
All accounting software packages offer online chat support	
Data can be processed more efficiently and accurately	✓
Invoices and statements can be generated automatically	✓
It removes the threat of viruses	
It reduces the likelihood of mathematical errors	✓
Data can easily be exported to other programs	✓
The Data Protection Act is no longer a consideration	

📖✏ Case study activity 7

	✓
With cloud-based accounting software, it is not necessary to be in the office as applications can be accessed anywhere on any device, as long as there is an internet connection. This means greater flexibility and easier access to data.	✓
Updates are not as easy and are more expensive with cloud-based accounting systems. Furthermore, the user needs to remember to run the updates, unlike 'off the shelf' packages where updates are automatic and quicker.	
'Off the shelf' accounting software often comes with much better support – this is available 24 hours a day, 7 days a week, via online chat communities and therefore is better suited for those working long hours.	
Traditional accounting software can prove more expensive, as there are both set up costs and the additional upgrade costs. Cloud-based software is usually paid for by a monthly subscription, so although there is a contract, the fee is fixed.	✓
All accounting functions can be accessed via the cloud and therefore it is easier for everyone to access the data, including customers and individuals with no connection to the company. Everyone has the same level of access, which is fairer.	

Case study activity 8

She should use:

d)   4yXkj2fR!*

Case study activity 9

Statement	Threat
Enters your computer from infected files or programs	**Viruses**
Enters your computer through emails	**Phishing**
Can trace every stroke of a key you make on your computer	**Hacking**

An introduction to Sage software

3

Introduction

To complete this unit you will need to be familiar with using one of the established accounting software products. Although many other computerised accounting packages are available, this Study Text will use the most popular for AAT studies, **Sage 50 Accounts**.

There are a number of versions of Sage - here we will primarily use **Sage 50 Accounts 2011.** This is an 'off the shelf' integrated computerised software package for accounts. Although Sage have developed a cloud-based alternative (SageOne), Sage Line 50 is accessed via a disc or licence and you will need a copy of this software to undertake the exercises in the case study part of this book.

If you have another version of Sage, or even another accounting package, you should still be able to proceed without too much difficulty, although you may find that some of the screen-shots used differ.

KNOWLEDGE	CONTENTS
There are no specific learning outcomes from the Access Award in Accounting Software covered within this chapter, as it covers the setup of the accounting software which is not examinable. However, this chapter is essential as you need to be able to set up the software before you can post the transactions in the proceeding chapters which are required in the assessment.	1 Accounting documents 2 Batch control and coding 3 Sage software

1 Accounting documentation

1.1 Case study: an introduction

📖 Case study

TotalPhoto Ltd specialise in contemporary family photography, most of which takes place in their rented studio on a small industrial estate on the outskirts of town. In addition, they also undertake a varied and increasing range of contracted photography, including weddings, dance shows and football competitions. They also supply photography equipment to the public and other photographers.

TotalPhoto Ltd has four members of staff, excluding Chrissie. In addition to Matt and Stuart, there is Sarala, a part-time photographer, and Michelle, the administrator for the company.

Since looking into the various types of accounting packages available and the advantages and disadvantages of each, Matt and Stuart have decided that they are going to use Sage Line 50 to process financial information for the company. Matt and Stuart now require more timely financial information on which to manage the company and feel that Sage Line 50 will enable them to do this. Chrissie will be responsible for processing the day to day information and therefore you should perform all of Chrissie's tasks using Sage Line 50.

We will use 30th September 2017 as '**today's date**' which is the last day of the company's financial year.

1.2 Types of accounting documentation

Business organisations rely on relevant documentation to record the transactions that it undertakes. Without an appropriate piece of supporting documentation, there is no way of knowing what has been bought, from whom and for how much, nor indeed what has been sold.

With a high proportion of modern transactions being on credit, an accurate and comprehensive system of recording transactions is essential.

Accounting documents are referred to as '**Source documents**'.

These documents include:

- purchase orders
- delivery notes
- purchase invoices
- credit notes
- sales invoices
- remittance advices.

For example, if an organisation wishes to purchase a new computer printer, it may first raise a purchase order which is sent to the supplier. The supplier would issue or deliver the printer along with a delivery note, to record the safe receipt of the goods. A supplier invoice requiring payment would follow. If the printer was faulty, it could be returned and a credit note issued. When the payment is sent it is accompanied by a remittance advice which itemises each transaction which is being paid.

This process and the nature of these documents are covered in more depth in Chapter 4, but these play an integral role in computerised accounting.

2 Batch control and coding

2.1 Batch control systems

In order for a transaction to be correctly recorded in a computerised accounting system, the appropriate documentation must first be raised and then the details entered into 'the system'. Rather than enter each document on to the computer as it is received, many organisations use a batch control system.

In a batch control system all similar documents are collected and processed together in one batch. For example, purchase invoices and sales invoices will be sorted into separate batches and each batch will be processed separately.

A batch control system will save time as the data processer is just focusing one task at a time.

2.2 Batch control sheets

Batch control can also help to make sure that computer entries are accurate.

First, a manual calculation is made to total each batch of documents. These totals are then checked against the computer system.

🔍 Definitions

Net amount - the total value of goods and services supplied, after discount and before VAT.

VAT (Value Added Tax) - A consumer tax collected by businesses on behalf of the government.

Gross amount – the total cost due from the customer including VAT.

💡 Example

Akddus works in the accounting department of Armistead & Co. One of Akddus' daily tasks is to make sure that all sales invoices notes are entered on to the computer.

Each day Akddus works through the previous day's sales invoices. He calculates the total net amounts, the total VAT amounts, and the total gross amounts. He then enters these totals on to a batch control sheet.

Today, Akddus has three invoices to process:

Armistead & Co

Ryan's Close

Lower Meltham

MT4 3SQ

Invoice no: 59870

Tax point: 16th June 2016

To: Pendleton Prisms
    Stuart Street
    Bristol, BR1 JQ8

	£
Goods	399.00
VAT 20%	79.80
Gross amount for payment	478.80

Payment terms: 15 days net

Armistead & Co

Ryan's Close

Lower Meltham

MT4 3SQ

Invoice no: 59871
Tax point: 16th June 2016

To: Wiggins Plc
    Prism Lane, Huddersfield, HT1 JQ3

	£
Goods	3,500.00
VAT 20%	700.00
Gross amount for payment	4,200.00

Payment terms: 15 days net

Armistead & Co

Ryan's Close

Lower Meltham

MT4 3SQ

Invoice no: 59872
Tax point: 16th June 2016

To: Dribbles Ltd
    Dowsett Street, Farnborough, FG6 5AD

	£
Goods	85.60
VAT 20%	17.12
Gross amount for payment	102.72

Payment terms: 30 days net

Akddus calculates the total net amounts, total VAT amounts, and total gross amounts and enters the figures on to a batch control sheet.

Sales invoice batch totals	Total net amounts £	Total VAT amounts £	Total gross amounts £
Tuesday 16th June 2016	3,984.60	796.92	4781.52

Akddus checks that the net amount and VAT amounts equal the total on the batch control sheet: 3984.60 + 796.92 = 4782.52

Akddus then enters the batch of invoices on to the computer and checks that the totals are the same as the figures on his batch control sheet.
Note: The process of how to do this is covered in Chapter 5.

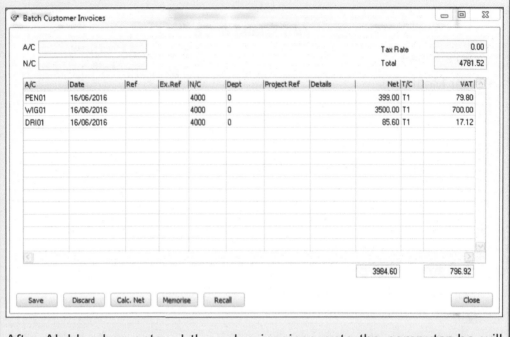

After Akddus has entered the sales invoices onto the computer he will check that the computer-generated batch totals match the total on the batch control sheet. If the totals are not the same, Akddus should check both the batch control totals and the computer entries and find the discrepancy before saving any of the data on the computer.

2.3 Coding

All computerised accounting systems work by the use of codes. Each supplier and each customer must be given a unique code by which the computer software can recognise them. It is vital that there can be no confusion between two suppliers with similar names. For example, you may be fully aware that John Green and John Greenwood are entirely different people, but it could be easy for a computer to mix them up. Each must therefore be given a unique code by which they can be identified.

Similarly, each product manufactured or sold by an organisation may be given a unique code. Also, employees are usually 'coded' – you could check your pay slip to find your own Employee Reference Number.

Finally, every type of income or expense, asset or liability, is given a unique code to identify it. It is essential that items entered into the accounting records are coded to the correct category - this ensures they are found in the correct place within the financial statements. We covered classification in Chapter 1, so make sure that when posting transactions, you pay attention to what it is you are posting.

For example, if you buy a new car, this is classified as an asset and should therefore be coded in the assets section of the nominal i.e. Motor Vehicles; it should not be posted to Motor Vehicle Expenses. Coding makes entering transactions quite straightforward, you need only refer to the relevant four digit code rather than a long narrative description. Coding on Sage Line 50 will be covered in more detail in Chapter 4.

Codes must be unique. However, they should also be recognisable by the person dealing with the system. For example, if a supplier was coded "SMITH006", this would be far more recognisable than a purely numeric code such as "0827329".

Care must be taken to issue codes that are not ambiguous. The use of a combination of letters and numbers (an alphanumeric code) often achieves this.

In Sage, when you create a new customer or supplier record, the program will automatically suggest a code for that supplier. It does this by taking the first eight characters of the name. The suggested code for a customer called Greenwood would therefore be "GREENWOO". You may decide this is not the most appropriate code (think what the problem might be if you had two different suppliers called Greenwood), in which case you can easily change it. Many organisations have a set structure for coding, and if this is the case in your organisation you should follow it.

3 Sage Software

3.1 Installing Sage

Although you will not be required to install Sage as part of the AAT assessment, it is important to understand the initial installation process that will enable you to start using 'Sage 50 Accounts Professional' for the first time as part of your Computerised Accounting studies.

When you load Sage for the first time you should see the following screen:

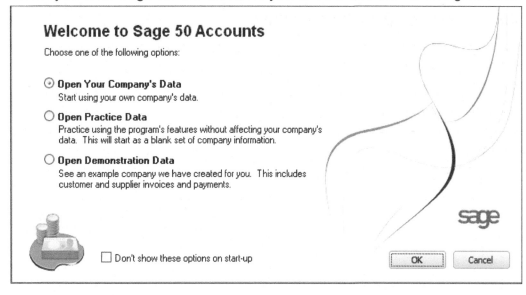

Welcome to Sage 50 Accounts

Choose one of the following options:

◉ **Open Your Company's Data**
Start using your own company's data.

○ **Open Practice Data**
Practice using the program's features without affecting your company's data. This will start as a blank set of company information.

○ **Open Demonstration Data**
See an example company we have created for you. This includes customer and supplier invoices and payments.

☐ Don't show these options on start-up   OK   Cancel

Assuming you are entering a new company (as you will be doing here, make sure that the "Open Your Company's Data" is marked. Don't worry at this stage about the other options – just press the [OK] button.

You should now see this screen:

Sage Accounts - Company Set-up

1 Welcome	**Welcome to Sage 50 Accounts** ?
	Please select one of the following to set-up a new company in Sage 50 Accounts:
	⊙ Set-up a new company ?
	○ Use an existing company stored on your network ?
	○ Restore data from a backup file ?
	Your company will be created in the following location. To choose a different location, click Change.
	C:\PROGRAMDATA\SAGE\ACCOUNTS\2012\COMPANY.002 [Change]

[Cancel]   [Back] [Next]

Your choice here depends on whether you are setting up a new company, or uploading existing data.

For now, you will be starting with a completely new company, so click on the "**SET UP A NEW COMPANY**" button as shown.

Once you have company details set up and saved in Sage, it will default to that company each time you start up. However, it is easy to return to this point if you wish to enter a new company.

3.2 Setting up a new company

When you start using Sage for your case study company, you must firstly enter some information about the company itself.

This is important because it will identify this particular company and appear on various reports. In addition, at this stage, you must enter the dates of the company's financial year. This is vitally important, as Sage will use this information in producing your annual accounts.

You will need the following information for this session:

Case study

Company Name:	TotalPhoto Ltd
Company Address:	Unit 63
	Bailey Industrial Estate
	Fornby Road
	Miltonby
	Lancashire
	LD37 7QZ
Telephone:	01949 969 378
Fax:	01949 969 379
E-mail:	info@totalphotoltd.webnet.uk
Website:	www.totalphotoltd.co.uk
Company Reg. Number:	376 096 823
VAT Number:	734928107
Accounting Period:	1st October – 30th September

Now we can begin entering the data for our company, TotalPhoto Ltd.

Case study activity 10

Enter the information onto the computerised system using the information provided in the previous box. Guidance follows.

Step One – Initial set up

You will be requested to complete the company details using the information given above.

As you enter the details, be sure to check for accuracy – but do not worry if you make a mistake because you can always amend it later (we will look at how you can amend errors in a later chapter).

Once you are happy with your entries click on the [Next] button.

Step Two – Selecting the business type

On this screen you can choose a business type for your business, this amends the nominal codes so they are specific for your business. For this exercise we are going to choose the Limited Company type.

Click the next button [Next]

Step Three – Entering the details of the Financial Year

This is a really important stage. You need to enter the dates of your company's Financial Year. Remember, for TotalPhoto Ltd the company's Financial Year is 1st October to 30th September.

Sage Accounts - Company Set-up

1 Welcome	**Select Financial Year** ? ?
2 Company Details	Choose when your company financial year begins. If you are not sure when your financial year begins, please contact your accountant for guidance before you proceed any further.
3 Business Type	Month	October
4 **Financial Year**	Year	2016
5 VAT	**Financial year range**
6 Currency	01 October 2
7 Confirm Details	

Click on the small arrow and a list of months will appear which you can select by highlighting. The same is true for the Year, which for the case study should be set as 2016.

Cancel   Back   Next

The data in this manual all refers to the year 2016-17, and so our Financial Year will start in **October 2016**. Enter this, using the drop down boxes. In the real computer based test you will be asked to decide on a suitable year to use based on the dates given. You will need to be consistent throughout the test to ensure your dates are correct.

Again, when you have done this press the [Next] button.

Step Four – Entering the VAT Details

Enter the VAT Registration Number as provided in the data (the number is *376096823*). The standard VAT rate is 20%.

Sage Accounts - Company Set-up

1 Welcome	**Select VAT Details** ?
2 Company Details	Is your company VAT registered? ⊙ Yes ○ No
	Enter your VAT registration number 376096823 ?
3 Business Type	VAT Scheme Standard VAT ?
4 Financial Year	Enter your standard VAT rate % 20.00 ?
5 **VAT**	
6 Currency	
7 Confirm Details	

Step Five – Entering the currency details

At this stage you can enter the currency details. All of TotalPhoto Ltd's transactions take place in the UK, so their base currency is "Pound Sterling". You should check that this option is correctly checked.

Again, click the [Next] button to proceed.

Note: During your studies relating to accounting software as part of the AAT qualification, you will not be required to deal with any currency other than £ Sterling.

Step Six – Confirming the information

At this stage is very important that you check the details you have entered so far.

If you are happy with the details, click the [Next] button to confirm.

1 Welcome	**Create** ?
2 Company Details	You must confirm that the key details below are correct. Click Back to make changes or click Create to create your company.
3 Business Type	**What you have entered**
	Data location: C:\PROGRAMDATA\SAGE\ACCOUNTS\2012\COMPANY.002
4 Financial Year	Share this folder? No
5 VAT	Company Name: TotalPhoto Ltd
	Business Type: Limited Company
6 Currency	Financial Year: 01 October 2016 - 30 September 2017
7 **Confirm Details**	VAT Scheme: Standard VAT
	Currency: Pound Sterling

Step Seven – Active Setup

You have now set up Sage with the basic information needed for the company TotalPhoto Ltd. The name of the company should appear at the top of the screen, with the dates at the bottom.

3.3   Navigating Sage

When you open Sage you will see the screen on the following page.

This 'window' (or screen) is the one that will now appear every time you open Sage. You will explore it in more detail as you progress through this Study Text. For now, just take the time to familiarise yourself with this screen. You can also change the view of the screen to different options by clicking on 'change view' which will be at the top right hand side of your screen.

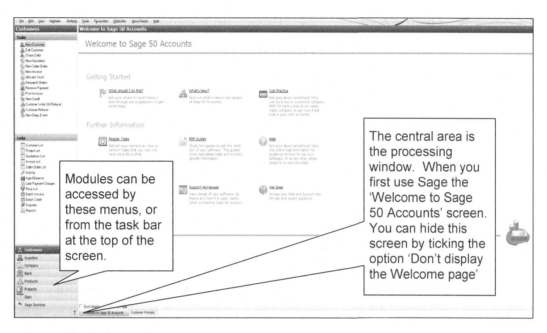

The central area is the processing window. When you first use Sage the 'Welcome to Sage 50 Accounts' screen. You can hide this screen by ticking the option 'Don't display the Welcome page'

Modules can be accessed by these menus, or from the task bar at the top of the screen.

3.4 Modules

Sage uses modules to differentiate different transactions. As you move through the different modules the processing area, tasks, and links will change depending on which module you are working on.

The modules that you will be using for the assessment are: Company and Bank. We will also explore the Customers and Suppliers module to familiarise you with these as they will be useful if working in an accounting environment.

The table below identifies the modules you will be using in the AAT assessment, the accounting term typically used for the module, and the main tasks which are carried out in each module.

Module	Ledger term	Main tasks
Customers	Sales Ledger	<ul><li>Enter and amend customer details</li><li>Enter sales invoices</li><li>Enter sales credit notes</li><li>Produce invoices and statements</li><li>Produce customer reports</li></ul>*In the AAT assessment, you may not be required to enter any Customer transactions.*
Suppliers	Purchase Ledger	<ul><li>Enter and amend supplier details</li><li>Enter purchase invoices</li><li>Enter purchase credit notes</li><li>Produce supplier reports</li></ul>*In the AAT assessment, you may not be required to enter any Supplier transactions.*

Company	Nominal or General ledger	• Enter and amend nominal account records • Produce nominal ledger account reports
Bank	Cash book	• Enter receipts from cash and credit customers • Enter payments to cash and credit suppliers. • Produce reports

You will be exploring these modules in more detail as you work through the case study.

3.5 Checking your data

If you work steadily and carefully, you should not encounter many problems with your data entry. However, no matter how carefully you work, you will undoubtedly have to make corrections at some time – either because of human error in inputting data, or simply because new information comes to light.

One important feature of Sage is the ability to check your data. This will help to identify any issues with data corruption (which can occur after a power cut, for example), missing data and date errors.

You can access the DataCheck facility by clicking on **FILE** in the main menu bar, then **MAINTENANCE**, and then **CHECK DATA.**

Sage will check the validity of your data and advise you of any possible discrepancies.

Check Complete ☒

No problems to report on data files.

OK

You should note that the DataCheck facility will **not** identify data entry errors (e.g. entering the wrong amount or posting to the wrong nominal code). The accuracy of data entry is your responsibility, and you should therefore aim to minimise the number of errors you make by being careful to check your work at all stages.

3.6 Making corrections

Many people are understandably a little nervous when using a computer system for the first time. They worry that they may break the system, or make mistakes that cannot be corrected.

Do not worry: Sage offers a number of easy ways to amend or delete errors. However, a full record of all amended or deleted transactions are maintained for audit trail purposes.

These are covered in a later chapter so do not panic if you do something wrong. You are only practising at this stage, and it is good to make mistakes initially as you will learn how to correct them! You are allowed to amend errors in the AAT assessments and will not be penalised for doing so. We all know that mistakes happen in the workplace and errors are often rectified.

3.7 Backing up your work

It is important that you save your data regularly to guard against accidental losses which can prove very costly and time-consuming to recover or re-input. Backing up your data should become part of your daily routine.

To back up data follow the following steps:

Step One

From the File menu at the top of the screen select 'Backup' (ignore the figures in the screenshot below as they are included for demonstration purposes only).

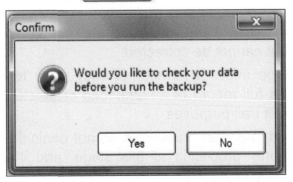

Sage now asks if you would like to check your data before you run the backup – you should select [Yes]

Hopefully there are no problems with your data files and so you will now be able to backup your data.

File maintenance

Error checking

Your data was last checked on:
18/10/2009. It is recommended you run this
option on a regular basis.

Check Data

Corrections

This option allows you to edit or correct
transactions already entered.

Corrections

ReIndex Data Files

This option allows you to create new
indexes for your ledger files.

ReIndex

Data compression

If you have previously deleted large
amounts of data, run this option to reclaim
disk space used by deleted records.

Compress Data

Rebuild new data

Choose this option to erase data files and
start from scratch. Use with extreme
caution.

Rebuild

Close

From this screen press the [Close] button to begin backup.

Backup

| Backup Company | Advanced Options | Previous Backups |

Company Details

You are about to create a backup of:

Company Name: TotalPhoto Ltd

Found In: C:\PROGRAMDATA\SAGE\ACCO

Where do you want the company backed up to?

We have suggested a filename and location to
with this suggestion click OK. If not enter a file
location for your backup.

Backing Up to removable media? Insert th

Backing Up to CD? Refer to the Help

Filename : totalphoto 19-10-20 .001

Location : C:\Users\

Browse...

Select the location to
back up your data here.
Most hard-drives begin
with a C:\. A memory
stick or other memory
device may be on the D,
E or other drive. Use the
BROWSE button to
check what devices are
available

OK   Cancel   Help

You need to select an appropriate file name – here, the name of our Case Study firm TotalPhoto Ltd has been used. Select **OK** to back up. The screen will now show a "Backup" box which indicates the progress of the backup. Another suggestion for a file name would be to include your name and this would be beneficial in the computer based test as it will help the assessor identity your work.

When this process has finished Sage will tell you that the backup has been successfully completed and you can click **OK**.

You should note as well that Sage invites you to back up your data each time you close the program down – the process is identical to that described above.

The nominal ledger

4

Introduction

The nominal ledger is probably the most important element of the Sage (or indeed any) accounting system.

This chapter focuses on the use of nominal codes and then how to enter and report on the information required. Within the AAT assessment you will be required to create new accounts in the general ledger and to amend existing ones.

We covered accounting terminology in Chapter 1, and it is important that you understand this to ensure that you create or amend accounts within the correct section of the Nominal Ledger.

KNOWLEDGE
Set up accounts
2.1 Create new accounts in the general ledger
2.2 Amend existing accounts in the general ledger

CONTENTS
1 Introduction
2 Entering a nominal code
3 Entering an opening balance
4 Creating a journal for initial capital
5 Printing reports

1 Introduction

1.1 Case study: an introduction

> 📖 **Case study**
>
> TotalPhoto Ltd have now set up their accounting software and the necessary staff members, including Chrissie, have received some external training from Sage to show them how to use the program.
>
> Chrissie has now been tasked with setting up and amending accounts within the general ledger to reflect the required information of the company.
>
> You should complete the tasks set throughout this chapter as if you are Chrissie.

1.2 The importance of the nominal ledger

The nominal ledger is probably the most important element of the Sage (or indeed any) accounting system. The key aspect to this is the list of nominal codes. This is simply a series of different accounts which are used each time a transaction is recorded.

Each of these accounts is given a unique four digit code number. To view the list of Nominal Codes go to the **Company** screen, and then **Nominal Ledger.** Then select **'List'** from the layout menu.

1.3 Nominal codes

This now shows you a list of all of the nominal codes (N/Cs) for the business:

The four-digit code is important, as the list is actually broken down into groups:

0000-0999	Fixed Assets and Depreciation (e.g. Buildings, Equipment)
1000-1999	Current Assets (e.g. Stock, Debtors, Bank)
2000-2999	Liabilities (e.g. Loans, Creditors)
3000-3999	Capital and Reserves
4000-4999	Sales
5000-5999	Purchases
6000-6999	Direct Expenses (e.g. Direct Labour)
7000-7999	Miscellaneous Overheads (e.g. Phone, Rent, Postage)
8000-8999	Bad debts and Depreciation
9000-9999	Suspense and Mispostings

Sage uses these 'groupings' of codes to ensure that items appear in the correct part of the Income Statement or Statement of Financial Position. You may have heard of these financial statements referred to as a 'Profit and Loss Account' or 'Balance Sheet'.

For the purpose of this assessment, you need to know that the Income Statement (Statement of Profit and Loss) shows all of your Income and Expenses therefore anything that is posted to nominal account codes

4000 and above, will be included in your Statement of Profit and Loss. Examples of items contained within the Statement of Profit and Loss include, sales, purchases and expenses.

The Statement of Financial Position shows all of your Assets, Liabilities and Capital and Reserves. This means that anything that you post to nominal codes 0000 – 3999 will be included in your Balance Sheet. Examples of items contained within the Statement of Financial Position include, Motor Vehicles, Loans, Capital and Drawings.

In Sage, you can easily amend the description of a nominal code, or indeed add a new one. However, you must always make sure that you keep the code in the correct 'grouping' for the type of account that it is, otherwise whatever you post to that nominal code could end up on the wrong Financial Statement when it comes to producing year-end accounts.

There may be some accounts used within the exam that you may not be familiar with in terms of the terminology or what it is. For example, the Prepayment account. You may be asked to post something to this account but you don't necessarily need to know what it is as this is covered later on in your AAT studies. To make it easier to locate a nominal code by name, you can sort the list into alphabetical order by clicking on the **Name** tab at the top of the list.

If you press **P** on your keyboard, it will take you straight to all the nominal accounts whose name begin with the letter P. If you scroll down, you will be able to locate the **'Prepayment'** nominal account.

You can easily change the list back to numerical order by clicking on **N/C** tab at the top of the list.

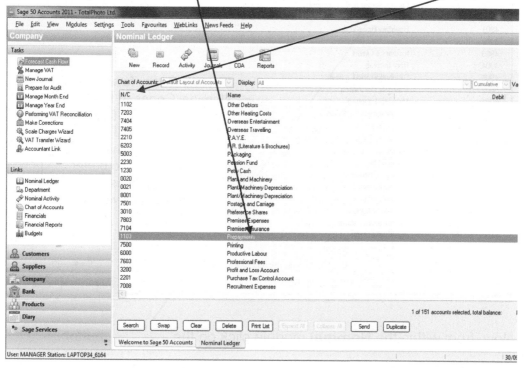

2 Entering a nominal code

2.1 Amending and creating specific nominal codes

The default Chart of Accounts contains the most common codes set up for a general business. However, you will almost certainly want to add to, or amend, these Nominal Codes to suit your business in particular.

For example, in your case study TotalPhoto Ltd you will want to be more specific when recording its sales and purchases. Before you do this, have a look at your listing of Nominal Codes. Find the 5000-5999 Range (remember, these are set aside for Purchases).

Nominal Ledger   (All Records) • Change View ▼ ✕

New   Record   Activity   Journals   COA   Reports

Chart of Accounts: Default Layout of Accounts ▼ Display: All ▼ Cumulative ▼ Variance: Don't Show ▼ Layout: List ▼

N/C	Name	Debit	Credit
4400	Credit Charges (Late Payments)		
4900	Miscellaneous Income		
4901	Royalties Received		
4902	Commissions Received		
4903	Insurance Claims		
4904	Rent Income		
4905	Distribution and Carriage		
5000	Materials Purchased		
5001	Materials Imported		
5002	Miscellaneous Purchases		
5003	Packaging		
5009	Discounts Taken		
5100	Carriage		
5101	Import Duty		
5102	Transport Insurance		
5200	Opening Stock		
5201	Closing Stock		
6000	Productive Labour		
6001	Cost of Sales Labour		
6002	Sub-Contractors		

> There are very few general Nominal Codes in this range, from 5000-5999. TotalPhoto Ltd will need to be able to create new codes within this range to better reflect the activities of the business. Details will be provided later.

0 of 150 accounts selected, total balance: Debit   0.00   Credit   0.00

Search   Swap   Clear   Delete   Print List   Expand All   Collapse All   Send   Close

Now, from within the **Nominal** module click on the   Record   button.

You should now have a blank record screen, as below.

Nominal Record -

Details   Graphs   Activity   Memo

N/C   [▼]
Name   [   ]
Balance   0.00   Account Type   [   ]

Month	Actuals	Budgets	To end Sep 2009
B/F	0.00	0.00	0.00
Oct	0.00	0.00	0.00
Nov	0.00	0.00	0.00
Dec	0.00	0.00	0.00
Jan	0.00	0.00	0.00
Feb	0.00	0.00	0.00
Mar	0.00	0.00	0.00
Apr	0.00	0.00	0.00
May	0.00	0.00	0.00
Jun	0.00	0.00	0.00
Jul	0.00	0.00	0.00
Aug	0.00	0.00	0.00
Sep	0.00	0.00	0.00
Future	0.00	0.00	0.00
Total	0.00	0.00	0.00

Save   Discard   Delete   Previous   Next   Print List   Close

To **AMEND** an existing code:

- Enter the Nominal Code (or select from the pull down menu)

- Type in the new name

To **CREATE** a new code:

- Enter the new Nominal Code (making sure it is in the correct range)

- Type in the new name

There is also the option of using a 'wizard' to set up a new nominal code. It is a very straightforward process and it guides you through the relevant steps. To do this, click on **Company** and then **New**.

This screen will appear; you click next and fill in the details to set up your new account. Once you have completed all of the relevant details within the wizard, you click finish to save the details within your nominal coding list.

📖✎ Case study activity 11

Chrissie now understands how to amend and create Nominal Codes. She must enter each of the following N/Cs and names. She needs to do them one by one, and save each one.

SALES		PURCHASES	
Nominal Code	Name	Nominal Code	Name
4000	Sales – Individuals & Family	5000	Purchases – Film
4001	Sales – Weddings	5001	Purchases – Paper
4002	Sales – Corporate	5002	Purchases – Cartridges & Toner
4003	Sales – Nurseries & Schools	5003	Purchases – Stationery
4004	Other sales	5004	Purchases – Other Consumables

Once you have created and amended the nominal codes from the previous activity, close down the window and generate the Nominal List report for the range 4000-5999.

First click on 🗐 Reports at the top of the screen. Then select **Nominal Details reports** and then double click **Nominal List.**

KAPLAN PUBLISHING

This screen will then appear; enter the nominal range that you want to show in your report i.e. **4000** and **5999** and click ok.

Criteria for Nominal List		
Criteria Values		
Enter the values to use for the criteria in this report		
Nominal Code	Between (inclusive) ▾ 4000 ▾ and 5999 ▾	
Preview a sample report for a specified number of records or transactions (0 for all)	0	
Help	OK	Cancel

The report should look like this:

Date: 13/01/2018   **TotalPhoto Ltd.**   **Page:** 1
Time: 21:29:43   **Nominal List**

N/C From: 4000
N/C To: 5999

N/C	Name
4000	Sales - Individuals and Family
4001	Sales - Weddings
4002	Sales - Corporate
4003	Sales - Nurseries & Schools
4004	Other Sales
4009	Discounts Allowed
4099	Flat Rate - Benefit/Cost
4100	Sales Type D
4101	Sales Type E
4200	Sales of Assets
4400	Credit Charges (Late Payments)
4900	Miscellaneous Income
4901	Royalties Received
4902	Commissions Received
4903	Insurance Claims
4904	Rent Income
4905	Distribution and Carriage
5000	Purchases - Film
5001	Purchases - Paper
5002	Purchases - Cartridges & Toner
5003	Purchases - Stationery
5004	Purchases - Other Consumables
5009	Discounts Taken
5100	Carriage
5101	Import Duty
5102	Transport Insurance
5200	Opening Stock
5201	Closing Stock

Note the new sales categories here

Note the new purchases categories here

Case study activity 12

To help Chrissie locate nominal codes as she continues to use Sage, she now prints out a list of all nominal codes. She can do this by following the same process as above but entering the range 0000 – 9999 or simply pressing the Print List button located towards the bottom of the screen. The full list of default Nominal Codes will then print.

This list should be kept safe, as it will be used when entering transactions in the future.

(The list is given in the answers section at the end of this chapter).

3 Entering an opening balance

3.1 Entering an opening balance

Case study

Having successfully completed the activities, Chrissie can now amend or create new nominal codes. She has also printed a list of nominal account codes.

She now needs to enter the opening balances for each of the accounts relating to TotalPhoto Ltd on the Sage accounting software system.

Case study activity 13

Chrissie needs to enter the opening balances for the accounts on the first date she used the Sage software to record financial transactions for the company. For TotalPhoto Ltd, this is the 30th September 2017.

All balances will need to be posted as either a **DEBIT** balance (on the left hand side) or a **CREDIT** balance (on the right hand side).

1   Chrissie will need to create a new Nominal Code for Photographic Equipment.

2   Chrissie should also re-name the following nominal accounts:

• Petty Cash (1230) to 'Cash Account'

- Sales Tax Control Account (2200) to 'VAT on sales'
- Purchase Tax Control Account (2201) to 'VAT on purchases'
- Ordinary Shares (3000) to Capital introduced
- Preference Shares (3010) to Drawings

Chrissie must be very careful to enter each balance correctly as either a **debit** or a **credit** balance. Taking her time to complete this will prevent errors at this stage.

(Note: In the AAT assessment, you will be told in the assessment whether each of the balances are debits or credits, it is important that you enter these onto the correct side of the nominal account in order to get it right.)

Chrissie is provided with the following information to enter the opening balances for some of TotalPhoto Ltd's accounting:

TotalPhoto Ltd

Opening Balances

	Nominal code	Debit	Credit
Bank Current Account	1200	668.80	
Cash Account	1230	252.00	
VAT on sales	2200		369.36
VAT on purchases	2201	382.56	
Capital introduced	3000		1000.00
Purchases – Film	5000	1568.90	
Purchases - Stationery	5003	343.90	
Sales – Individuals & Families	4000		565.80
Sales – Weddings	4001		328.50
Sales – Corporate	4002		952.50
		3216.16	**3216.16**

(A step by step guide follows to help you complete this activity)

Step One

From the main screen click on the '**Company**' button. This will bring up the Nominal Ledger screen.

Step Two

Highlight the Nominal Code for which you want to enter an opening balance.

The first amount we need to enter is a debit balance of £668.80 for Bank Current Account (1230). Double-click your mouse on this code.

Now click on the 'Opening Balance (**OB**)' icon.

Having done so, keep the Ref as "O/Bal". The date in the 'Date' box should be the 30th September 2017; you should enter the opening balance amount of £668.80 in the Debit box. Leave the credit box at zero. Then click the **Save** button.

Notice how the detail record for Nominal Code 1200 (Bank) has now changed, showing your entry in September. When you return to the Nominal Ledger page you should also see the new balance reflected there.

Follow the same process to enter all the other opening balances for TotalPhoto Ltd.

4

Creating a journal for initial capital

4.1 Creating a journal

Case study activity 14

On 15th September, 2017 Matt Evans, one of the directors of TotalPhoto Ltd invested some additional capital of £2,000 into the firm.

The amount that Matt has invested will be put into the bank account, so Chrissie needs to increase the figure in the bank account and increase the amount of capital invested.

A journal is created to record this transaction in both accounts.

	Debit	Credit
Bank current account	2,000.00	
Capital introduced		2,000.00

(Step by step guidance on how to complete this activity follows below)

4.2 Guidance for Activity 14

Step One

From the main screen click on the **Company** button. This will bring up the Nominal Ledger screen. Then click on the **Journal** icon in the task bar or task list.

Step Two

In the Journal task screen enter the following details:

- Enter **J001** as the reference to identify this as the first journal transaction that has been processed in the computerised accounts system.

- The Posting date is the date of the transaction: **15/09/17**

- Enter the journal transaction as shown on the following screen. Make sure that you enter a narrative into the Details field so that the reason that this journal transaction was made can be identified at a later stage.

- Check that the total debits and credits should be the same, and the Balance remaining at the top of the screen should be 0.00

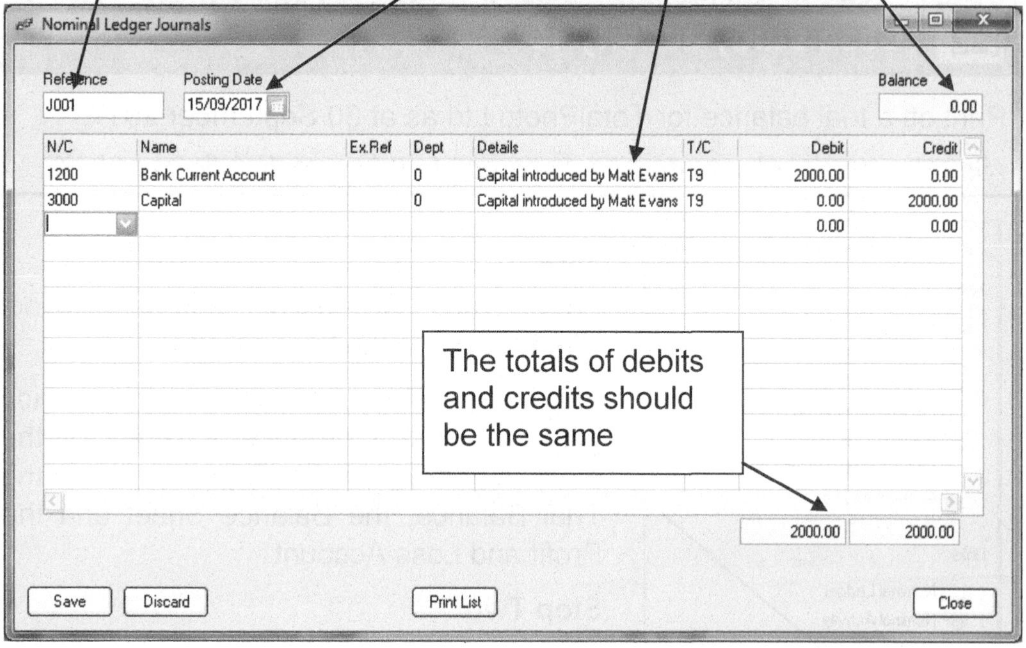

5 Printing reports

5.1 Printing the period trial balance

📖 Case study

Chrissie has now entered all the opening balances for TotalPhoto Ltd. The next step is for her to begin entering transactions on a day-to-day basis. Before doing this, she will print off a Trial Balance.

📖 Case study activity 15

Print off a trial balance for TotalPhoto Ltd as at 30 September 2017.

(Step by step guidance on how to complete this activity follows below)

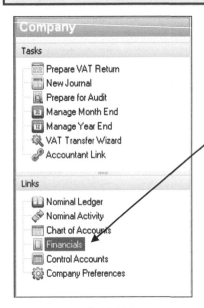

Step One

From the **Company** screen, select "**Financials**" in the links section.

This will create a new screen, from which you can quickly produce a series of the most useful reports in Sage, including the Trial Balance, the Balance Sheet and the Profit and Loss Account.

Step Two

From the toolbar at the top of the Financials screen, select the "**Trial**" icon

Step Three

You are now asked to select how you want to print the report.

For now, you will just preview the report (i.e. view it on screen).

Highlight this and the press the [Run] button.

Print Output

Output
- ○ Printer
- ⊙ Preview
- ○ File

[Run] [Cancel]

Step Four

As you want to view the trial balance as at September 2017, to see the opening balances you have entered, make sure you amend the date box to show September 2017.

Leave the next box as 0, and click OK.

Criteria for Period Trial Balance	X

Criteria Values

Enter the values to use for the criteria in this report

Period	To (inclusive)	12: September 2017

Preview a sample report for a specified number of records or transactions (0 for all) |0|

Help	OK	Cancel

Step Five

This should bring up a trial balance showing balances for the period up to September 2017. You may need to maximize the screen to see the whole report on screen – do this by clicking the *maximize* icon in the top right corner of the window (□)

If you have entered everything correctly you should see that both columns (debit and credit) balance to £5,216.16 and there should be no account called 'Suspense' in the list.

Step Six

You should now print out this trial balance and keep it safe.

This shows what your trial balance should look like after entering all of the opening balances:

Date:	13/01/2018	**TotalPhoto Ltd.**		Page:	1
Time:	22:17:13	**Period Trial Balance**			

To Period: Month 12, September 2017

N/C	Name	Debit	Credit
1200	Bank Current Account	2,668.80	
1230	Cash Account	252.00	
2200	VAT on Sales		369.36
2201	VAT on Purchases	382.56	
3000	Capital		3,000.00
4000	Sales - Individuals and Family		565.80
4001	Sales - Weddings		328.50
4002	Sales - Corporate		952.50
5000	Purchases - Film	1,568.90	
5003	Purchases - Stationery	343.90	
	Totals:	5,216.16	5,216.16

5.2 How to amend an incorrect opening balance

> 📖 **Case study**
>
> Having printed off the trial balance, Chrissie realises that it does not balance and therefore she has entered some data incorrectly. She remembers the training she received and does not panic and amends the incorrect opening balance accordingly.

If you enter an opening balance incorrectly or if any of the balances on your Trial Balance are different to the ones in the activity, you are able to amend as follows:

- Firstly, tick off your trial balance figures against the figures in the activity to determine which opening balances have been entered incorrectly and make a note of them.

- Go to the '**Company**' screen and find the first incorrect nominal ledger account in the list and double click on it.

- Then click on '**OB**'.

You will then need to decide what it is required to amend the incorrect balance. For example, if you had entered the bank current account as £688.80 Dr as opposed to the correct balance of £668.80 Dr, you would need to credit the account with £20.00 to reduce it to the correct figure. To do this, you simply enter 20.00 in the credit box and then click ok. The same process would be followed if you needed to increase your figure; you would simply enter the difference on the same side as the original figure and click ok.

If you prefer, you could reverse your original entry by doing the exact opposite of what you did originally. In the example error above, enter an opening balance of £688.80 Cr and that will revert the account back to its original nil balance. You can then repeat the step with the correct figure on the correct side to make it right.

After you have amended and saved any incorrect balances you can print off another Trial Balance and tick it off to check that it is correct.

Answers to chapter activities

📖 Case study activity 12

The list should look like this:

Date:	13/01/2018	TotalPhoto Ltd.	Page:	1
Time:	21:35:07	Nominal List		

N/C From: 0000
N/C To: 99999999

N/C	Name
0010	Freehold Property
0011	Leasehold Property
0020	Plant and Machinery
0021	Plant/Machinery Depreciation
0030	Office Equipment
0031	Office Equipment Depreciation
0040	Furniture and Fixtures
0041	Furniture/Fixture Depreciation
0050	Motor Vehicles
0051	Motor Vehicles Depreciation
1001	Stock
1002	Work in Progress
1003	Finished Goods
1100	Debtors Control Account
1101	Sundry Debtors
1102	Other Debtors
1103	Prepayments
1200	Bank Current Account
1210	Bank Deposit Account
1220	Building Society Account
1230	Petty Cash
1235	Cash Register
1240	Company Credit Card
1250	Credit Card Receipts
2100	Creditors Control Account
2101	Sundry Creditors
2102	Other Creditors
2109	Accruals
2200	Sales Tax Control Account
2201	Purchase Tax Control Account
2202	VAT Liability
2204	Manual Adjustments

For other activities in this chapter, the guidelines provided in the step by step instructions and accompanying screenshots will ensure successful completion of the tasks.

Setting up suppliers and customers

5

Introduction

Business organisations will use computerised accounting systems to keep records of all their suppliers and customers.

The organisation will need to keep very accurate and timely records of all transactions with their suppliers and customers. These transactions will typically include:

1) Invoices and credit notes

2) Payments made to suppliers and monies received from customers.

In addition, it would be very convenient to have all the contact details of each supplier and customer easily to hand.

Fortunately, Sage provides a very comprehensive management system which covers all these requirements (and more). You will see how this works shortly, but firstly you will need to enter your suppliers' and customers' details.

KNOWLEDGE	CONTENTS
There are no specific learning outcomes covered within this chapter as it covers the setup of customer and supplier accounts which is not examinable. However, knowledge of this process is useful if you are thinking of undertaking a role which involves computerised accounting.	1 Supplier details 2 Customer details

1 Supplier details

1.1 Case study: an introduction

> 📖 **Case study**
>
> Now that the Nominal Ledger has been set up, Chrissie has been asked to set up accounts for some of TotalPhoto Ltd's credit customers and suppliers.
>
> You should complete the activities throughout his chapter as if you were Chrissie.

1.2 Suppliers

> 🔍 **Definition**
>
> A **supplier** is an individual or organisation providing goods or services to another in exchange for money.
>
> Therefore, all of the suppliers relating to the TotalPhoto case study will be companies or individuals who sell and deliver products or services to TotalPhoto Ltd.

> 📖 **Case study activity 16**
>
> Chrissie is required to set up six of TotalPhoto Ltd's suppliers on the Sage system. The details for these suppliers are given below.
>
> She must first set up Mackay Films Ltd onto her accounting software system.
>
> Their details are as follows:
>
> | **Mackay Films Ltd** | **A/c Ref : MF001** |
> |---|---|
> | 33 West Parade | Tel 01828 827493 |
> | Miltonby | Contact: Carl Richardson |
> | Lancashire | Credit Terms: **30 days** |
> | LN87 7HD | Nominal code: 5000 |
>
> *(Follow the step by step instructions below to set up this supplier)*

1.3   Entering supplier details

Step One

From the Supplier Process window (below) select the new supplier wizard by clicking on either **'New Supplier'** in the Tasks list, or on the **New Supplier icon**.

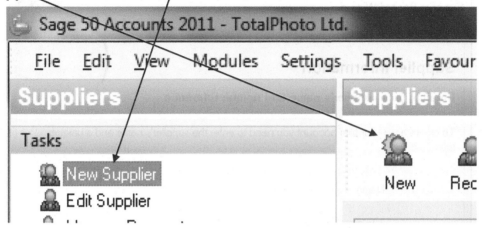

This will bring up the **Supplier Record Wizard**, which will help you to easily enter your suppliers' details.

Step Two

To complete the first screen of the **New Supplier Wizard** you will need to enter the supplier's name (Mackay Films Ltd) and their unique Account Reference Number (A/C Ref – MF001).

This is seen on the following page.

The Account Reference Number is a shorthand way of identifying each of your suppliers. You can use this code on documentation, and also it will appear on reports that you will print out.

It is extremely important that the number you choose is unique and it is useful if it helps to identify the supplier in some way – here MF001 representing **M**ackay **F**ilms.

Step Three

It is important to check your spelling for accuracy as errors (although they can be rectified) can cause confusion.

Note: The Account Reference Number cannot be changed after any transactions have been entered on to the account. Check carefully that you have entered the correct code for the account.

If you are happy press the [Next] button to move on.

Step Four

You now need to enter the supplier's address, telephone and fax details.

Again, when you are happy, press [Next]

Step Five

Now you can enter the firm's contact details. In this case we have not got an e-mail or website address, or the VAT number. Do not worry, though, as these can easily be entered at a later date.

You can enter Carl Richardson's name at this point though.

Step Six

The next screen asks you to enter details of any discount available from this supplier, the nominal code against which purchases from this supplier will be recorded, and also the most common VAT rating for the goods that you buy from them.

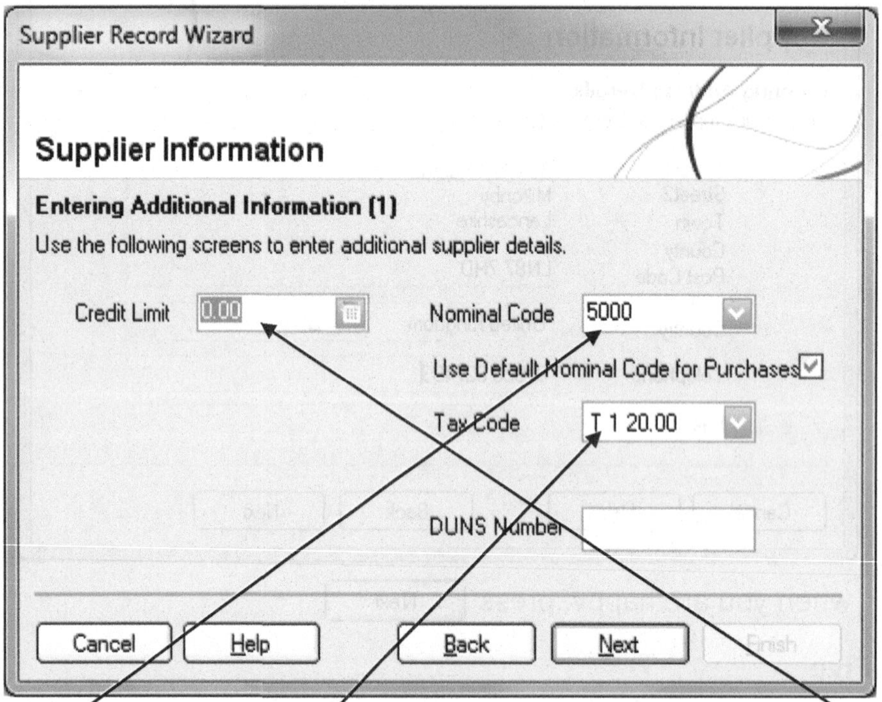

Supplier Record Wizard

Supplier Information

Entering Additional Information (1)

Use the following screens to enter additional supplier details.

Credit Limit 0.00   Nominal Code 5000

Use Default Nominal Code for Purchases ☑

Tax Code T 1 20.00

DUNS Number

| Cancel | Help | Back | Next | Finish |

Mackay Films Ltd do not offer any discount, so this can be left at **0.00.**

The firm supplies films to TotalPhoto, so the **Nominal Code** should be **5000**.

The VAT code is **T1**, meaning that the majority of purchases from this supplier will have VAT added at 20%.

If you are happy with this press the [Next] button.

Step Seven

Now you can enter credit details agreed with this supplier.

- **Credit limit** is the amount of credit allowed by this supplier. In this instance, we have not been given any details so **leave this as zero**.

- **Settlement Due Days and Sett. Disc** % relate to any extra discount allowed by the supplier if the invoice is paid within a certain time. In this instance, no settlement (or cash) discount has been given, so **leave both these boxes as zero.**

- **Payment Due Days** are the credit terms that the supplier offers. Most suppliers will insist on payment within a certain period of time – typically seven to twenty eight days **(the payment due days).**

However, some suppliers may also offer a discount for payment within an earlier period **(the settlement due days)**.

Mackay Films Ltd offer credit terms of **30 days** meaning TotalPhoto Ltd must pay invoices within 30 days after the invoice date.

- **Terms** Enter the terms agreed as text: 30 days.

- **Terms agreed** This box should be ticked as this tells Sage that the details have been confirmed. If you forget to do this at this particular stage, don't worry as you can choose to tick terms agreed by double clicking on the particular supplier in the **SUPPLIERS** module, and then clicking on the 'credit control' tab.

Note: The date to use for opening balances can differ to the 'today's date' given in the scenario. Therefore, always read the wording carefully to ensure you use the correct date.

Supplier Record Wizard	X

Supplier Information

Entering Additional Information (2)

Settlement Due Days	0	Sett.Disc %	0.00
Payment Due Days	30		
Terms			
Terms Agreed	✓ ?		

Cancel	Help		Back	Next	Finish

Step Eight - A/C Opened

For the TotalPhoto Ltd Case Study we are working in the month of September, 2017. Any new accounts opened this month will be dated the 1st September, 2017.

On the following screen either type the date (30/09/2017) or use Sage's calendar facility to enter it, as shown below. The date of the **Next Credit Review** can be left blank and the **Credit Ref** can be left blank.

Supplier Record Wizard	X

Supplier Information

Entering Additional Information (3)

Please enter additional information about the supplier.

Credit Ref		A/C Opened	30/09/2017
		Next Credit Review	/ /
		Last Credit Review	/ /

| Cancel | Help | | Back | Next | Finish |

Check that the details you have entered into Sage are the same as the image on this page. If you are happy with this press the | Next | button.

Step Nine

The next two screens ask you to enter the details of your supplier's bank. This is essential if the business is paying their suppliers using methods such as BACS.

It is not necessary for you to do this in this example and you will not be required to in your AAT assessment so you can simply click | Next | to skip these screens.

Sage now asks if this supplier has an outstanding balance – in other words, if at the time of entering their details you already owe them money.

As all the TotalPhoto supplier accounts you are entering are new suppliers, click the option shown below.

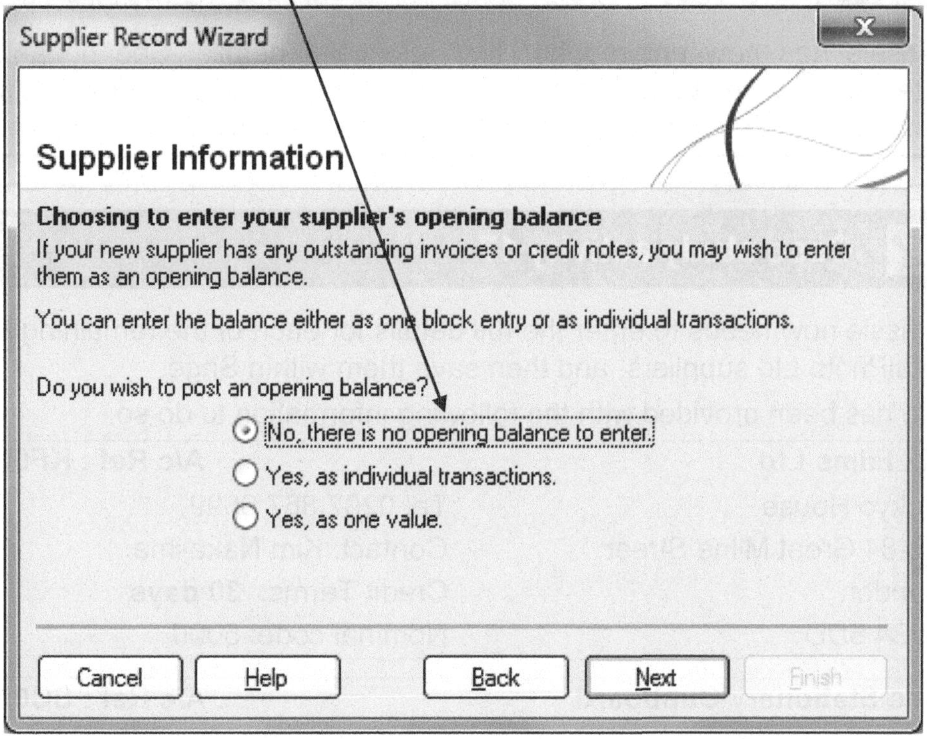

Supplier Record Wizard

Supplier Information

Choosing to enter your supplier's opening balance

If your new supplier has any outstanding invoices or credit notes, you may wish to enter them as an opening balance.

You can enter the balance either as one block entry or as individual transactions.

Do you wish to post an opening balance?

⊙ No, there is no opening balance to enter.

○ Yes, as individual transactions.

○ Yes, as one value.

| Cancel | Help | Back | Next | Finish |

Step Ten

Sage now confirms that you have successfully entered the supplier's details. The next stage is important – you **must** press the [Finish] button to save the details and to post the opening balance.

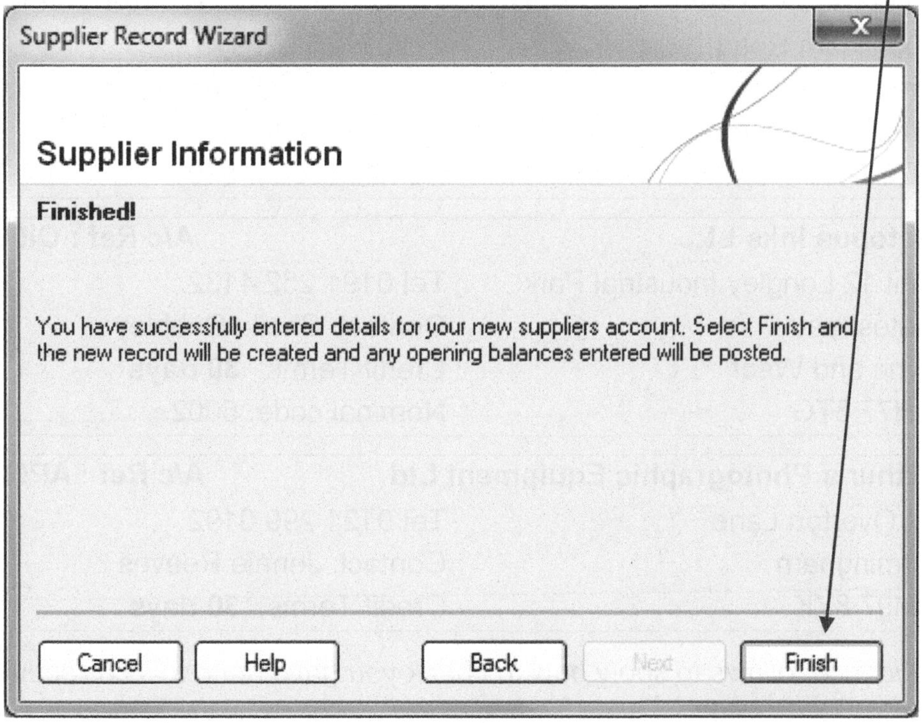

Supplier Record Wizard

Supplier Information

Finished!

You have successfully entered details for your new suppliers account. Select Finish and the new record will be created and any opening balances entered will be posted.

| Cancel | Help | Back | Next | Finish |

📖 Case study

Chrissie has now entered her first supplier's details. She began by entering their company details, such as their address, phone and fax numbers and then input the credit terms this supplier makes available.

📖 Case study activity 17

Chrissie now needs to enter the full details for each of the remaining five TotalPhoto Ltd suppliers, and then save them within Sage.

She has been provided with the following information to do so:

K2 Films Ltd	**A/c Ref : KF001**
Tokyo House	Tel 0207 867 6599
72-84 Great Milne Street	Contact: Kim Nakajima
London	Credit Terms: **30 days**
WC4 6DD	Nominal code: 5000

The Stationery Cupboard	**A/c Ref : SC003**
21 Potter Way	Tel 01482 417378
Hull	Contact: Alan Pensill
Humberside	Credit Terms: **14 days**
HU87 6YY	Nominal code: 5003

Mills Paper Products	**A/c Ref : MP002**
405 Ream Road	Tel 01726 378918
Bradford	Contact: Mr Shaun Squire
West Yorkshire	Credit Terms: **21 days**
BD5 6QA	Nominal code: 5001

Octopus Inks Ltd	**A/c Ref : OI001**
Unit 12 Longley Industrial Park	Tel 0191 252 4132
Gateshead	Contact: Sheila Cribbley
Tyne and Wear	Credit Terms: **30 days**
GH77 5TG	Nominal code: 5002

Arthur's Photographic Equipment Ltd	**A/c Ref : AP004**
77 Overton Lane	Tel 0121 299 0192
Birmingham	Contact: Jennie Reeves
BM97 8YK	Credit Terms: **30 days**

(Guidance follows to show how to check you have done this correctly).

KAPLAN PUBLISHING

To see a list of the suppliers you have entered, from the Supplier Process window **Change View** to 'Suppliers'.

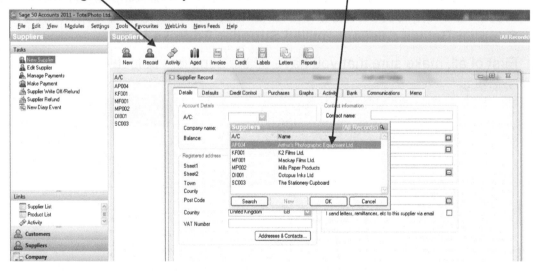

Your list of suppliers should look like this:

A/C	Name	Balance	Credit Limit	Contact	Telephone
AP004	Arthur's Photographic Equipment Ltd.	0.00	0.00	Jennie Reeves	0121 299 0192
KF001	K2 Films Ltd.	0.00	0.00	Kim Nakajima	0207 867 6599
MF001	Mackay Films Ltd.	0.00	0.00	Carl Richardson	01828 827493
MP002	Mills Paper Products	0.00	0.00	Mr Shaun Squire	07126 378918
OI001	Octopus Inks Ltd	0.00	0.00	Sheila Cribbley	0191 252 4132
SC003	The Stationery Cupboard	0.00	0.00	Alan Pensill	01482 417378

If you spot a mistake, you can go into the **Supplier Record** by clicking on the **Record** icon, then selecting the correct supplier from the dropdown and making the necessary corrections.

1.4 Printing supplier details reports

You have entered the details of the six suppliers, so let's now check that they are correct by running off a report from Sage.

The first report to print is the **Supplier List**.

To do so, from the **Suppliers** window (shown below), click on **Reports** in the **Links** area or the **Reports** icon

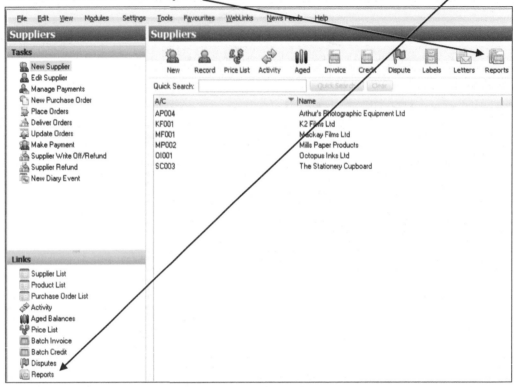

This will produce a new window with a list of supplier-related reports categorised by type of report. You will practice accessing some more of these later on, but for now the one that you want is a report in the **Supplier Details** category entitled **Supplier Address List.**

First of all, make sure that you have all the suppliers selected.

Double click on **Supplier Address List** to produce the report.

On the next screen you can identify the criteria by which you wish to select the contents of your report. As you wish to see a list of all the suppliers that you have entered keep the boxes as shown below, then press OK.

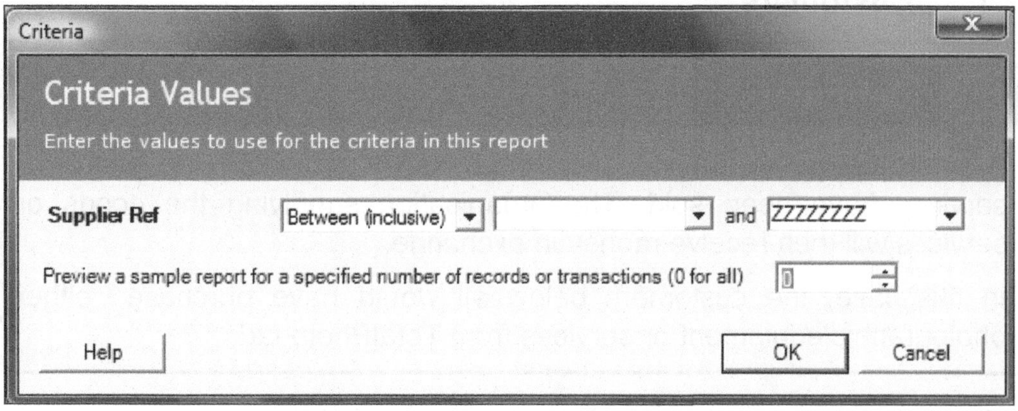

Criteria	X

Criteria Values

Enter the values to use for the criteria in this report

| **Supplier Ref** | Between (inclusive) ▼ | | ▼ | and | ZZZZZZZZ | ▼ |

Preview a sample report for a specified number of records or transactions (0 for all)   [0]   ⬍

| Help | | OK | Cancel |

Your report should now show on screen, similar to the one below. Remember, that you might be working on a different version of Sage but the main areas will be the same but possibly with a slightly different presentation.

Date:	14/01/2018		**TotalPhoto Ltd.**	
Time:	15:09:50		**Supplier List**	

Supplier From:
Supplier To: ZZZZZZZZ

A/C	Name	Contact	Telephone
AP004	Arthur's Photographic Equipment Ltd.	Jennie Reeves	0121 299 0192
KF001	K2 Films Ltd.	Kim Nakajima	0207 867 6599
MF001	Mackay Films Ltd.	Carl Richardson	01828 827493
MP002	Mills Paper Products	Mr Shaun Squire	07126 378918
OI001	Octopus Inks Ltd	Sheila Cribbley	0191 252 4132
SC003	The Stationery Cupboard	Alan Pensill	01482 417378

There are many other supplier reports available in this section, we will go through some of them later on in the book but for now, you should feel confident enough to access the reports listing and from here, you can print them out.

The exact list of reports that you will use will depend on your particular requirements.

You will feel much more comfortable in generating reports once you have practised clicking through the different ones and seeing what information they contain, so have a go!

2 Customer details

2.1 Customers

🔍 Definition

A **customer** is an individual or organisation to whom the goods or services have been sold. The organisation supplying the goods or services will then receive money in exchange.

In this case, the customers below all would have purchased either photographic equipment or services from TotalPhoto Ltd.

2.2 Entering customer data

The process of entering your customers' details is very similar to that of entering supplier information, so you should feel confident doing this now.

Consistent, accurate recording of information is a vital aspect of any credit management system, ensuring that your organisation gets paid as quickly as possible for its sales. This can be the difference between failure and survival for most businesses.

We can now start to look at the 'Customers' process and begin with entering the initial information regarding our case study firm, TotalPhoto Ltd. Again, you will find detailed step by step instructions after this activity.

📖 Case study activity 18

TotalPhoto Ltd has six customers with outstanding balances as at 30th September 2017. Their details follow on the next page.

Chrissie needs to enter the first customer Mr W Haslam onto the system.

Note: Mr W Haslam opened his account on 01/09/2017

(Step by step guidance follows to show how to do this).

📖 **Case study**

TotalPhoto Ltd Customer details

Mr W Haslam 22 Brown Street Miltonby Lancashire LN87 6FD Credit terms: Payment in 14 days	**A/c Ref : HAS004**

Mrs H Poppy 120 Forrest Way Miltonby Lancashire LN87 9YR Credit terms: Payment in 14 days	**A/c Ref : POP002**

Mrs T Pashby 30A Andrews Street Killington Lancashire LN85 6TT Credit terms: Payment in 14 days	**A/c Ref : PAS002**

Campbell & Dunn Ltd 12 The Beeches Miltonby Lancashire LN87 9PP Credit terms: 14 days	**A/c Ref : CAM004**

Lullabies Nursery 104 Victoria Road Miltonby Lancashire LN87 5PS Credit terms: Payment in 14 days	**A/c Ref : LUL002**

Miss S Pargenter 11 Alexandra Park Miltonby Lancashire LN87 2WD Credit terms: Payment in 14 days	**A/c Ref : PAR006**

2.3 How to enter customer information

Step One

Go to the Customer screen, as below.

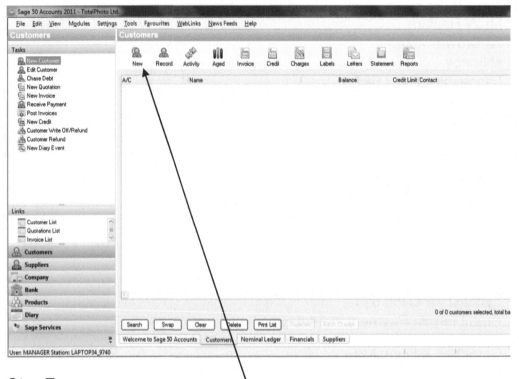

Step Two

From the Task Bar, click on **New Customer**. At the next screen click NEXT, and you should now be able to enter your first customer's details, as below.

Step Three

When you have done this click the **NEXT** button again, and enter the address details, as below.

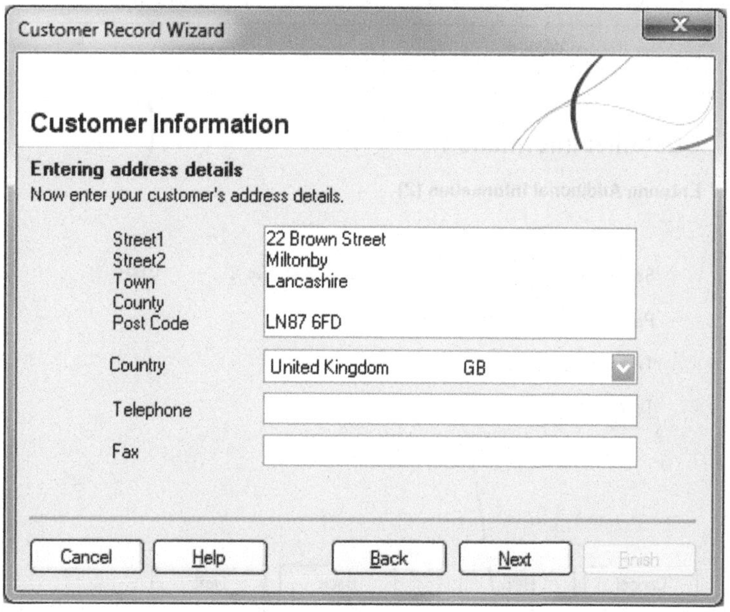

As with the supplier entry process, the next screen will ask you for further contact details, such as email and website addresses. You do not need to enter any information here at this point, so press the **NEXT** button.

Step Four

On the Customer Defaults screen, we will keep all the defaults, so you do not need to change anything.

Leave the nominal code as 4000, and the tax code as T1 (20.00), as in the screen above. You will learn more about these shortly.

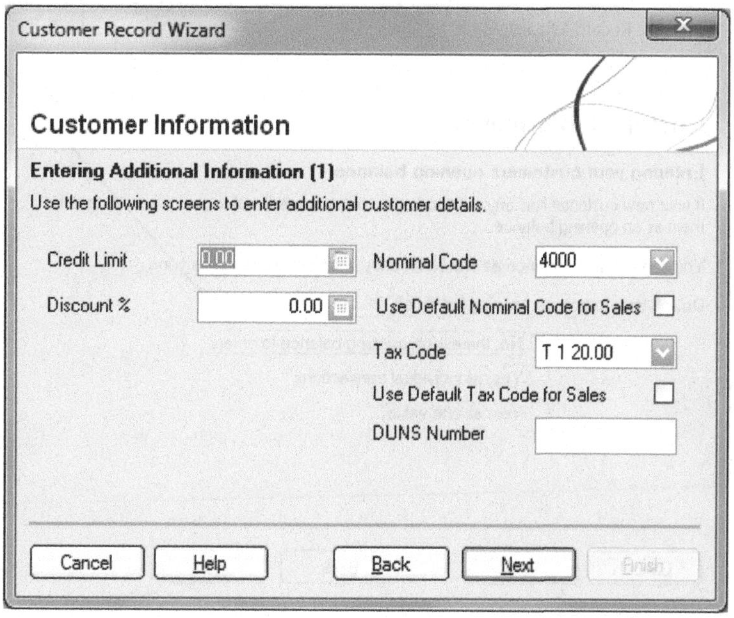

Step Five

Now you can enter the credit terms. For Mr Haslam we will require payment within fourteen days, and there is no settlement discount for early payment. Mr Haslam opened his account on 01/09/2017.

Step Six

Remember to tick the Terms Agreed box.

We do not have any bank information for Mr Haslam so we do not need to enter any details on the next two screens.

Step Seven

Sage will now ask if there are any opening balances, and as with the supplier entry screen there is no opening balance as this is a new account.

Step Eight

You can now **create** this account.

Step Nine

Click on the '**Finish**' button to complete the process.

📖📝 Case study activity 19

Chrissie has already entered one of TotalPhoto Ltd's customers (Mr W Haslam).

She should now enter the full details for each of the remaining five customers, and then save them to Sage. All accounts should be opened as at 1st September 2017.

When she has done this, her 'Customers' screen should look like this:

A/C	Name	Balance	Credit Limit	Contact
CAM004	Campbell & Dunn Ltd.	0.00	0.00	
HAS004	Mr W Haslam	0.00	0.00	
LUL002	Lullabies Nursery	0.00	0.00	
PAR006	Miss S Pargenter	0.00	0.00	
PAS002	Mrs T Pashby	0.00	0.00	
POP002	Mrs H Poppy	0.00	0.00	

(Guidance follows to show how to check you have done this correctly).

2.4   Printing customer data reports

You have entered the details of the six customers, so let us now check that they are correct by running off a customer details report from SAGE.

From the **Customers** window (shown below), click on **Reports** in the **Links** area or the **Reports** icon.

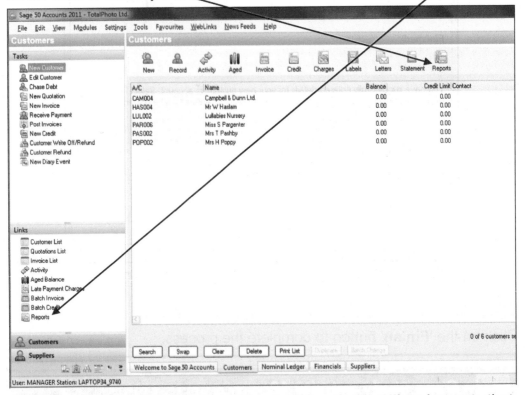

This will produce a new window with a list of customer-related reports that you may want to print and use. You will practice accessing some more of these later on, but for now the one that you want is the report entitled **Customer Address List.**

This is contained within the folder called **Customer Details Reports** – to access the contents of this (or any) folder simply click on the folder icon.

This is shown on the following page.

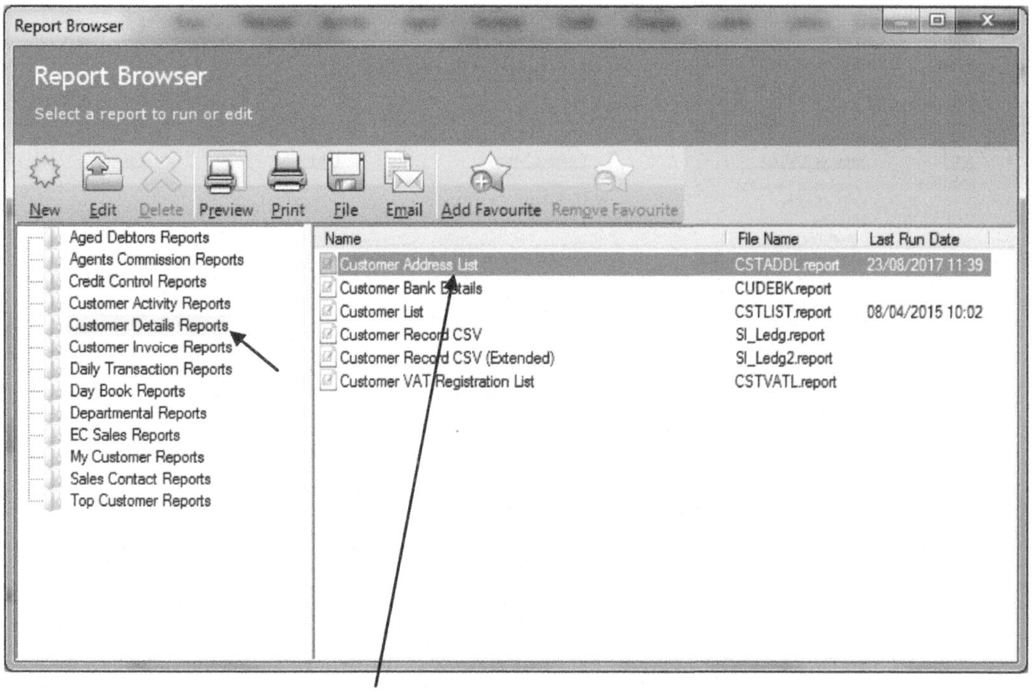

Double click on **Customer Address List** to produce the report.

On the next screen you can identify the criteria by which you wish to select the contents of your report. As you wish to see a list of all of the customers that you have entered keep the boxes as shown below, then press OK.

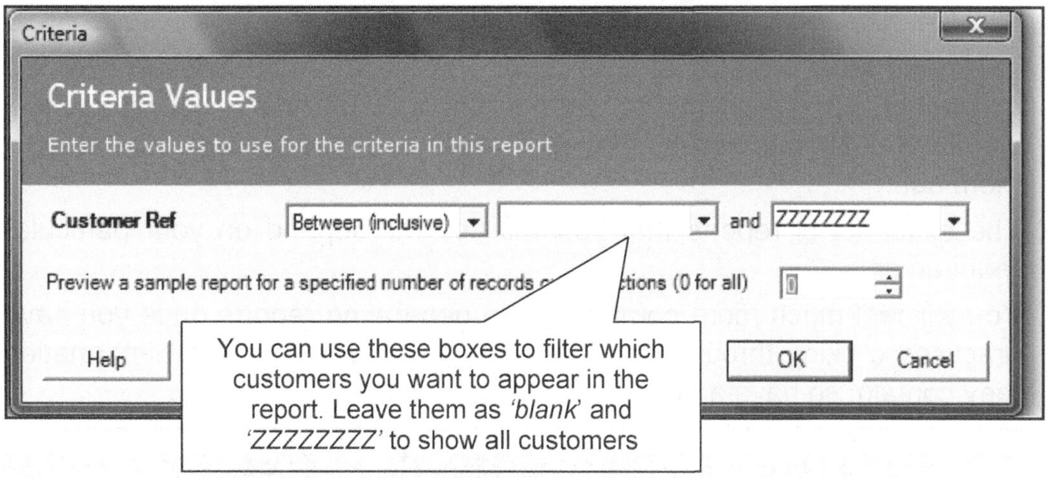

Your report should now show on screen, similar to the one on the following page.

| Date: | 22/01/2018 | **TotalPhoto Ltd.** | | Page: | 1 |
| Time: | 10:13:01 | **Customer Address List** | | | |

Customer From:
Customer To: ZZZZZZZZ

A/C	Name & Address	Contact Name	Telephone	Fax
CAM004	Campbell & Dunn Ltd. 12 The Beeches Miltonby Lancashire LN87 9PP			
HAS004	Mr W Haslam 22 Brown Street Miltonby Lancashire LN87 6FD			
LUL002	Lullabies Nursery 104 Victoria Road Miltonby Lancashire LN87 5PS			
PAR006	Miss S Pargenter 11 Alexandra Park Miltonby Lancashire LN87 2WD			
PAS002	Mrs T Pashby 30A Andrews Street Killington Lancashire LN85 6TT			
POP002	Mrs H Poppy 120 Forrest Way Miltonby Lancashire LN87 9YR			

There are many other customer reports available in this section - we will go through some of them later on in the book, but for now, you should feel confident enough to access the reports listing and from here, you can print them out.

The exact list of reports that you will use will depend on your particular requirements.

You will feel much more comfortable in generating reports once you have practised clicking through the different ones and seeing what information they contain, so have a go!

📖 Case study

Chrissie has now entered account details for six suppliers and six customers of TotalPhoto Ltd and has run the relevant reports to check her work. She is now feeling more comfortable with the accounting software.

The next step is for Chrissie to start entering transactions relating to these accounts.

Entering customer and supplier transactions

6

Introduction

As identified in the previous chapter, a computerised accounting system is required to record business transactions on a daily basis.

Having now set up customer and supplier records, this chapter will focus on the nature of credit transactions and how customer and supplier invoices and credit notes are processed using a computerised system.

KNOWLEDGE

There are no specific learning outcomes covered within this chapter as it covers processing customer and supplier transactions which is not examinable in the AAT Access Award in Accounting Software.

However, knowledge of this process is useful if you are thinking of undertaking a role which involves computerised accounting.

CONTENTS

1 Business transactions
2 Credit sales – customer transactions
3 Credit purchases – supplier documents

1 Business transactions

1.1 Case study: an introduction

📖 Case study

Now that Chrissie has set up accounts for TotalPhoto's credit customers and suppliers, she has been asked to process some financial information in relation to them. Chrissie is required to enter both customer and supplier invoices and credit notes onto the system.

You should complete the activities throughout his chapter as if you were Chrissie.

1.2 Cash and credit transactions

Any business will carry out a wide range of transactions every day of the week. The majority of these will fall into one of the following categories:

Credit transactions

- Purchases of goods and services credit
- Sales of goods or services on credit
- Payments made to suppliers (for goods/services bought on credit)
- Receipts from customers (for goods/services sold on credit)

Cash transactions

- Purchases made by cash/cheque/card
- Sales made for cash/cheque/card
- Payments made to meet other expenses
- Payment of salaries and wages to staff
- Petty cash transactions
- Transactions directly through the bank account (bank charges, interest, direct debits, standing orders)

Each of these transactions will have an effect on two accounts within the Sage system – this is the underlying principle of double-entry bookkeeping. However, Sage simplifies this by carrying out much of the double entry automatically.

Consider the first transactions – purchases and sales made on credit. This means that a legally binding contract is established between the two parties and the goods or services are supplied but payment is not paid until a later date. The key document in this process is the **invoice** – it demands payment and lays down the agreed terms of the transaction.

Hence, entering a credit transaction (whether a purchase or a sale) is a two stage process in Sage:

1   Enter the details of the invoice against the relevant supplier or customer. This will establish the presence and value of the legally binding debt.

2   At a later date, enter the details of the payment of the debt, either the payment sent to the supplier or the receipt received from the customer.

This approach is applicable for both credit sales and credit purchases – you just have to be sure to enter the details in the correct part of Sage.

1.3   Batch control

In order for a transaction to be correctly recorded in a computerised accounting system, the appropriate documentation must first be raised and then the details entered into 'the system'. Rather than enter each document on to the computer as it is received, many organisations use a batch control system.

In a batch control system all similar documents are collected and processed together in one batch. For example, purchase invoices and sales invoices will be sorted into separate batches and each batch will be processed separately. Similarly, documents recording receipts from customers will be separated from those that record payments to suppliers.

A batch control system will save time as the data processer is just focusing one task at a time.

Batch control is also useful to help to check that the entries made on the computer are accurate. First, a manual calculation is made to total each batch of documents. These totals are then checked against the computer system.

📖✎ **Case study activity 20**

Chrissie has been given six sales invoices to process using her accounting software package.

Date	Invoice No	A/c No	Customer	Nominal Code	Net Amount	VAT	Gross Amount
30/09/2017	4891	POP002	Poppy	4001	£105.00	£21.00	£126.00
30/09/2017	4892	HAS004	Haslam	4000	£24.50	£4.90	£29.40
30/09/2017	4893	PAR006	Pargenter	4000	£12.00	£2.40	£14.40
30/09/2017	4894	LUL002	Lullabies Nursery	4003	£100.00	£20.00	£120.00
30/09/2017	4895	CAM004	Campbell & Dunn	4002	£45.00	£9.00	£54.00
30/09/2017	4896	HAS004	Haslam	4000	£12.00	£2.40	£14.40

She must firstly calculate batch totals and record them on the following batch control sheet:

Batch Control Sheet – Sales Invoices

Sales invoice batch totals 30th September 2017	Total net amounts £	Total VAT amounts £	Total gross amounts £
Totals			

Having completed this activity, the details can be input on to Sage.

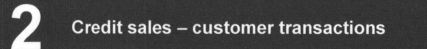

2 Credit sales – customer transactions

2.1 Entering customer invoices

📖✎ **Case study activity 21**

Chrissie is now required to enter each transaction onto the computer, making sure that the computer generated batch totals agree with the totals on the batch control sheet.

(Guidance on how to complete this activity follows below)

The easiest way to do this is to input all the invoices at the same time. To do this you will use the **Batch Customer Invoices** screen.

To enter a batch of customer (sales) invoices go to the '**Customers**' module and then press the '**Invoice**' button.

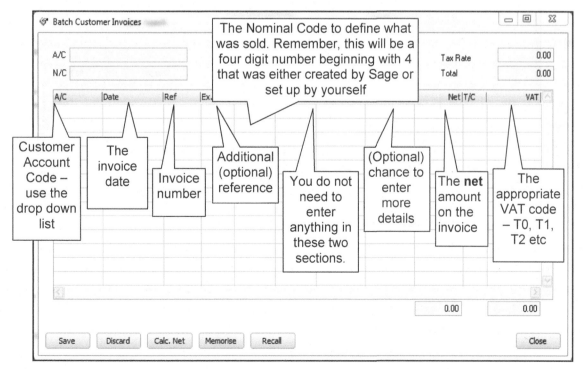

You can then insert data into the next screen as follows:

Once you have entered all invoices in the batch you should then review them to ensure you have entered them correctly, and then [Save] them.

This will post the invoices to Sage and update the system accordingly.

Case study activity 21 (continued)

Chrissie can now enter the six invoices for TotalPhoto Ltd using the batch invoicing method.

Enter the details in the batch customer invoices screen as shown below. You can choose suitable wording for the 'details' tab and a suggestion has been given for each.

When all six invoices have been entered, the screen should look like this:

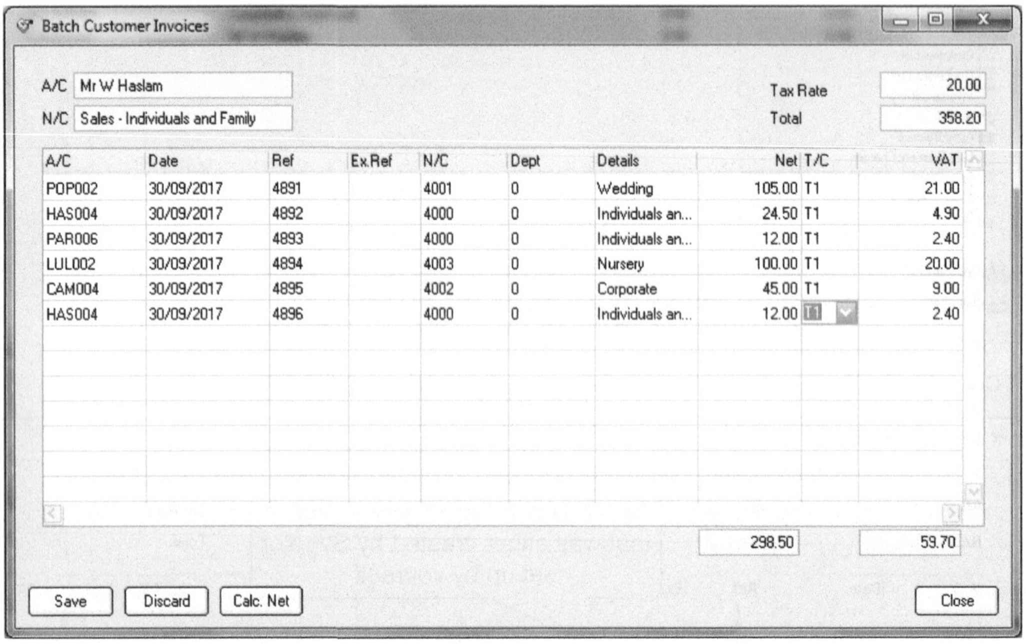

A/C	Date	Ref	Ex.Ref	N/C	Dept	Details	Net	T/C	VAT
POP002	30/09/2017	4891		4001	0	Wedding	105.00	T1	21.00
HAS004	30/09/2017	4892		4000	0	Individuals an...	24.50	T1	4.90
PAR006	30/09/2017	4893		4000	0	Individuals an...	12.00	T1	2.40
LUL002	30/09/2017	4894		4003	0	Nursery	100.00	T1	20.00
CAM004	30/09/2017	4895		4002	0	Corporate	45.00	T1	9.00
HAS004	30/09/2017	4896		4000	0	Individuals an...	12.00	T1	2.40

A/C: Mr W Haslam Tax Rate 20.00
N/C: Sales - Individuals and Family Total 358.20

298.50 59.70

[Save] [Discard] [Calc. Net] [Close]

Check that the Total Net figure, the Total VAT figure and the Total figure at the top of the screen all match the totals you wrote down on the Batch Control Sheet from Case Study Activity 20. If the totals do not match check that the entries you made on the computer are accurate.

When you are happy, press the [Save] button.

Case study activity 22

Chrissie now needs to print out another trial balance for September 2017 (she produced one of these earlier in Chapter 4). She should compare the two reports and identify the changes that have occurred.

(See below for how this should look if it has been completed correctly)

Here is a copy of how the Trial Balance should now look:

Date:	14/01/2018	**TotalPhoto Ltd.**		Page:	1
Time:	20:09:19	**Period Trial Balance**			

To Period:	Month 12, September 2017		

N/C	Name	Debit	Credit
1100	Debtors Control Account	358.20	
1200	Bank Current Account	2,668.80	
1230	Cash Account	252.00	
2200	VAT on Sales		429.06
2201	VAT on Purchases	382.56	
3000	Capital		3,000.00
4000	Sales - Individuals and Family		614.30
4001	Sales - Weddings		433.50
4002	Sales - Corporate		997.50
4003	Sales - Nurseries & Schools		100.00
5000	Purchases - Film	1,568.90	
5003	Purchases - Stationery	343.90	
	Totals:	5,574.36	5,574.36

2.2 Entering customer credit notes

A credit note is essentially a 'negative invoice' and is produced and sent to customers when a refund is needed. The most likely time this will happen is when goods that the organisation has sold to a customer have been returned as faulty. However, they can also be used to correct errors.

Producing a credit note in Sage is straightforward and effectively mirrors the process for producing an invoice.

Case study activity 23

The sale of a 6" × 4" colour print made by TotalPhoto Ltd to Mrs Poppy for £12.00 (plus VAT) is returned as faulty.

It is necessary for Chrissie to issue a credit note so that this debt is effectively 'removed' from Miss Poppy's account. The Credit Note No is 25 and the Nominal code to use is 4000, this should be dated 30th September 2017.

(Guidance on how to enter the credit note on Sage follows)

Step One

Complete the batch control sheet

Add up the figures in the Net Amount column, the VAT column and the Gross Amount column and enter the totals onto the batch control sheet:

	Total net amounts (£)	Total VAT amounts (£)	Total gross amounts (£)
Totals			

Step Two

Process the customer credit note

From the **Customer** module select **Customer List** and then from the

icons at the top of the screen select the [Credit] icon.

Here you can enter a batch of Credit Notes (just as you did with the batched invoices).

Sage shows your entries in RED to make it obvious that this is a Credit Note.

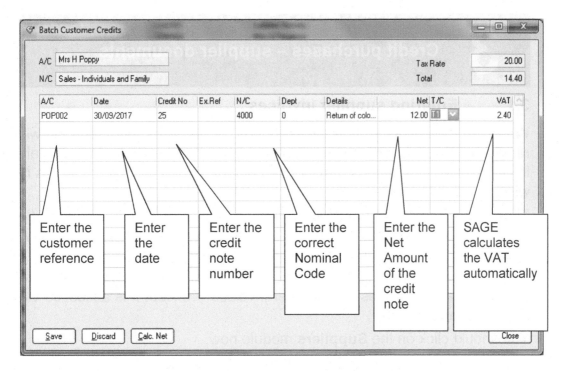

When you have entered all Credit Note(s) in the batch check the totals are the same as the batch control sheet then **SAVE** them to ensure that Sage can process them.

3 Credit purchases – supplier documents

3.1 Entering supplier invoices

When an organisation purchases goods or services on credit, it will receive an invoice from the supplier. These must be recorded immediately in Sage, even though they may not be paid for some time. We know this is when the business has purchased on credit, i.e. to pay later.

The most common way to process supplier invoices is to **batch** them (in much the same way as you did with the invoices to customers). This way, a number of invoices can be processed at the same time.

The process for entering batches of supplier statements is very similar to that for entering batches of customer invoices – except it is accessed via the **Suppliers** module.

You should click on the **Suppliers** module now.

Press the
Invoice
icon and enter the invoice details required.

Case study activity 24

TotalPhoto Ltd received the following five invoices on 30th September 2017.

Invoice Ref	Supplier	Account	Nominal Code	Gross Amount
1341	Mackay Films	MF001	5000	250.50
209	The Stationery Cupboard	SC003	5003	17.58
216	The Stationery Cupboard	SC003	5003	94.68
2203	Octopus Inks Ltd	OI001	5002	371.11
10092	Mills Paper Products	MP002	5001	195.02

You will notice that there is only the gross amount of each invoice listed in the table above. Sage will automatically calculate the VAT from the gross amount.

Chrissie needs to enter the five invoices on to the computerised accounting system.

(Step by step guidance follows to show how to enter the first invoice. Continue in the same way to enter the other four invoices in the batch. You can choose suitable wording for the 'details' tab - a suggestion has been given for each.)

Batch Control Sheet – Purchase Invoices

Purchase invoice batch totals 30th September 2017	Total net amounts (£)	Total VAT amounts (£)	Total gross amounts (£)
Totals			

When you have done the above activity the screen should look like this:

Enter all of the details into the necessary field on the screen, just as you did with the customer invoices.

When entering the figures, enter the **gross amount** into the **net column** and then click the **Calc Net** button at the bottom of the screen.

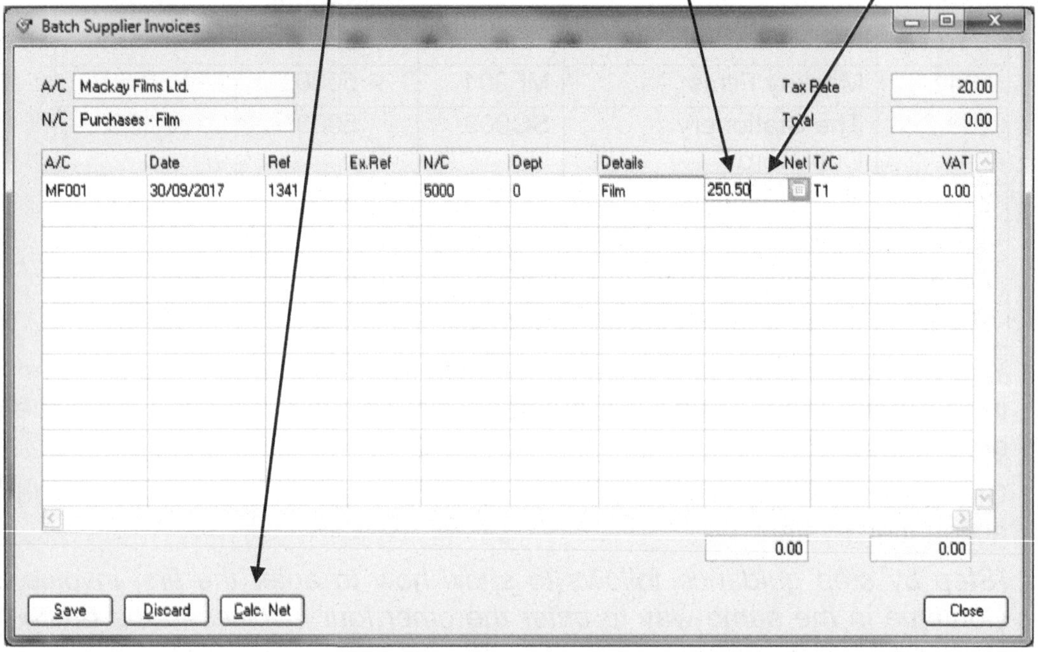

Sage will automatically split the gross figure into the net and VAT as shown below.

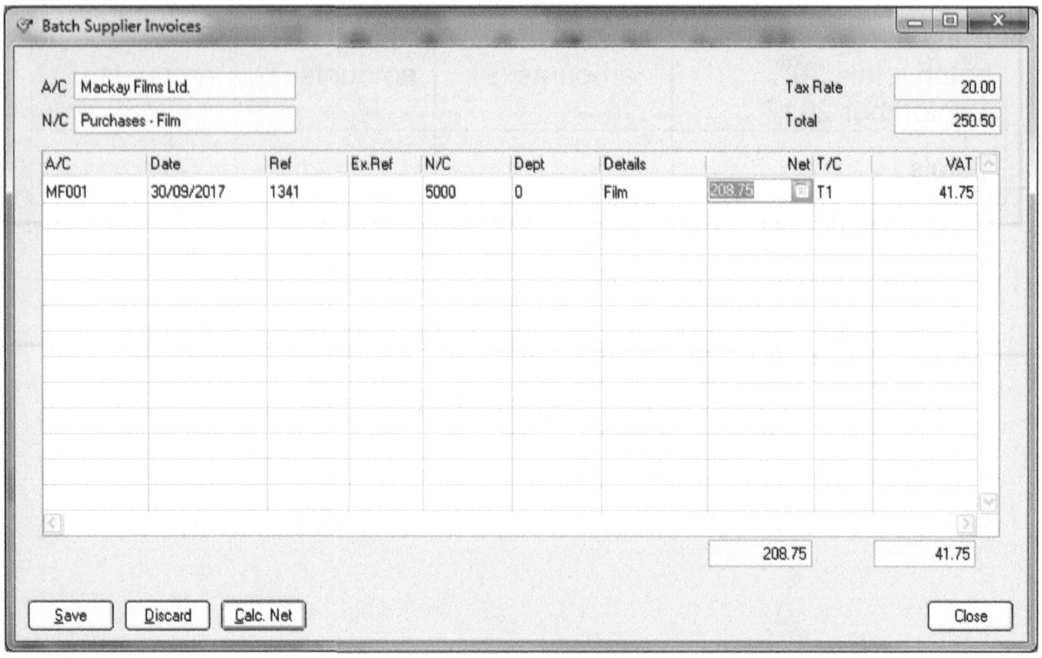

You should now post the remaining supplier invoices and once you have done this, your batch supplier invoices screen should look like this:

You should verify the entries and then press the **SAVE** button to post your entries to Sage.

Note: It is really important to pay attention to the amounts given to you in the AAT assessment to see whether they are inclusive or exclusive of VAT. You may be tested on this and entering data correctly into the system is key to passing the assessment. Remember, for any amount **including VAT** you must use the **Calc Net** button to split the VAT and net accurately.

3.2 Supplier credit notes

Supplier credit notes are processed in exactly the same way as you processed credit notes issued to customers. Access the entry screen from the **Suppliers** module using the **Credit** icon.

Case study activity 25

TotalPhoto Ltd receives one credit note.

It is from The Stationery Cupboard (Ref SC003) and is a credit for £14.65 (excluding VAT) because the incorrect goods were supplied. The credit note reference is 134C and it should be posted on 30/09/2017. The Nominal Code for this is 5003 (Stationery).

Chrissie is given the credit note for processing. She needs to:

a) Complete the batch control sheet

Batch Control Sheet – Purchase Credit notes

Purchase credit note batch totals 30th Sept 2017	Total net amounts £	Total VAT amounts £	Total gross amounts £
Totals			

b) Process the credit note using a suitable narrative for the details section (a suggestion has been shown).

Your entry screen for the above activity should look like this:

Note: Sage shows all of the above entries in red so that they are easily identifiable as a credit note. When you have checked the accuracy of your entries against the figures you entered in the batch control sheet you should press the **SAVE** button.

Having completed this, it is important to back up your work as covered in a previous chapter.

Processing credit payments and receipts

7

Introduction

This chapter looks at a second group of common business transactions, addressing the processing of receipts from credit customers and payments to credit suppliers.

KNOWLEDGE
There are no specific learning outcomes covered within this chapter as it covers how to process receipts and payments for credit customers and suppliers.
However, knowledge of this process is useful if you are thinking of undertaking a role which involves computerised accounting.

CONTENTS
1   Credit receipts
2   Credit payments

1 Credit receipts

1.1 Case study: an introduction

> ### 📖 Case study
>
> TotalPhoto Ltd have now received some money from some of their credit customers in respect of the invoices that Chrissie processed and from monies owed prior to this. Matt and Stuart have also made some payments to suppliers, the details of which he has passed on to Jessica to process using the Sage system.
>
> You should complete the activities throughout his chapter as if you were Chrissie.

1.2 Recording receipts from credit customers

Businesses will regularly receive monies from customers that have previously bought from them on credit.

> ### 📖 Case study activity 26
>
> On 30th September 2017, TotalPhoto Ltd also received two amounts from customers in respect of their outstanding invoices, a **receipts from customers listing** has been completed
>
> | Date | Receipt type | Customer | Amount (£) | Details |
> |------|-------------|----------|-----------|---------|
> | 30/09/17 | Cheque | Lullabies Nursery | 120.00 | Payment of Invoice 4894 |
> | 30/09/17 | Cash | Mrs H Poppy | 111.60 | Payment of Invoice 4891 and Credit Note 25 |
>
> Chrissie must enter these transactions onto a computerised system.
>
> *(Step by step guidance follows on how to complete this task on the computerised accounting system).*

To enter the receipt for Lullabies Nursery:

Step One

Click the on the **Bank** module, make sure that it is the **Bank Current Account** that is highlighted and then select **Customer** from the menu at the top of the screen.

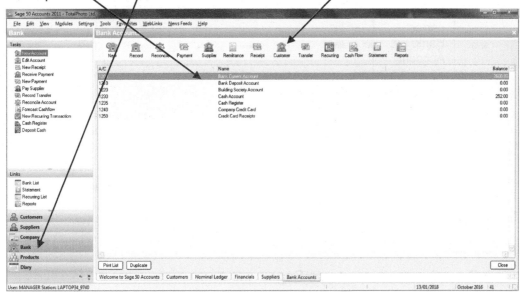

Step Two

In the top half of the screen in **Customer Details** search for the correct account, **LUL002** enter the date and the Reference.

At this stage do not enter the amount of the receipt

Note how Sage presents you with the outstanding invoices in the bottom half of the screen for the particular customer. This allows you to decide which outstanding invoices you want to pay.

Step Three

Enter £120.00 in the Receipt column for Invoice 4894 – this is the invoice being paid on this occasion.

Alternatively, you can click in the **receipt** box next to the invoice(s) that you would like to pay and click [Pay in Full], this will automatically enter the full amount of the invoice into the box.

Step Four

Click **Save** to post this entry to Sage.

Now enter the second receipt, from Mrs Poppy for £111.60.

This payment is to be allocated to two transactions on Mrs Poppy's account:

Sales invoice (SI) no 4891 for   £ 120.00

Sales credit note (SC) no 25 for £ _ 14.40

Total amount outstanding   £ 111.60

Open up their account as you did with the previous one. Your screen should look like this:

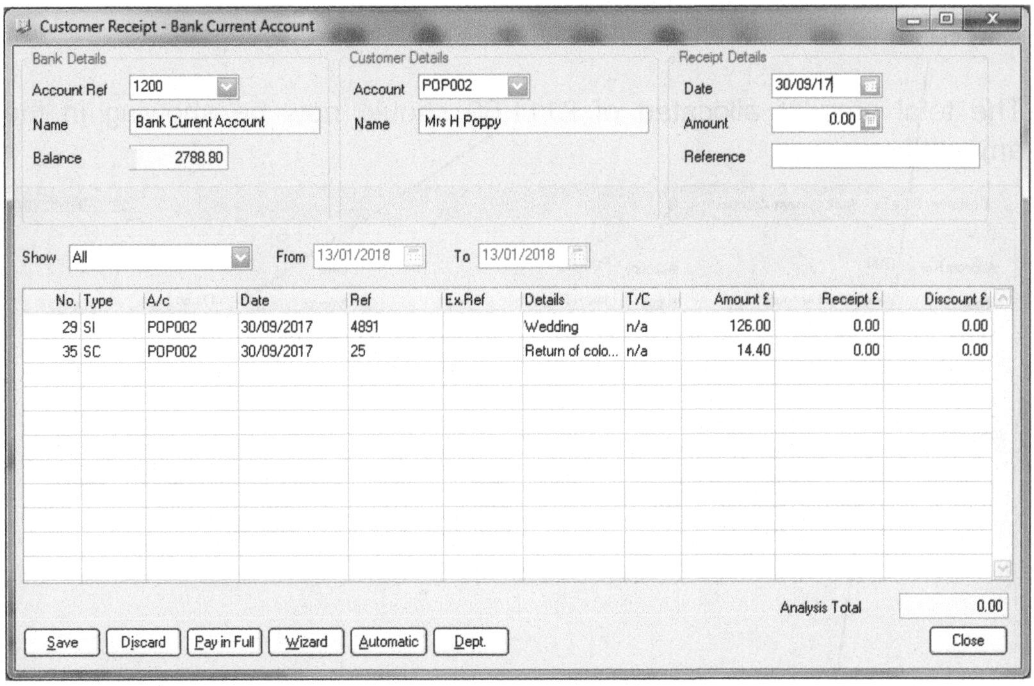

Enter the date and then the following screens will show you how to allocate this payment in two stages:

Step One

Go to the Invoice (SI) row then click on the receipt column and **Pay in Full**

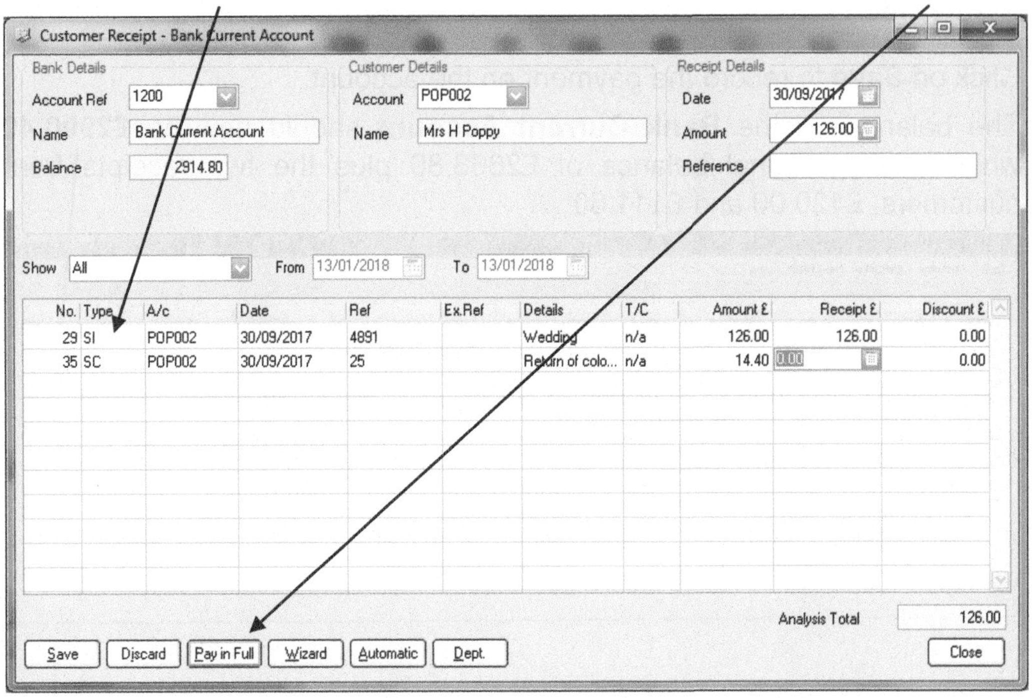

Step Two

Go to the Credit Note (SC) row then click on the receipt column and click

Pay in Full

The total amount allocated of £111.60 should now be showing in the amount box.

No.	Type	A/c	Date	Ref	Ex.Ref	Details	T/C	Amount £	Receipt £	Discount £
29	SI	POP002	30/09/2017	4891		Wedding	n/a	126.00	126.00	0.00
35	SC	POP002	30/09/2017	25		Return of colo...	n/a	14.40	14.40	0.00

Customer Receipt - Bank Current Account

Bank Details
Account Ref 1200
Name Bank Current Account
Balance 2900.40

Customer Details
Account POP002
Name Mrs H Poppy

Receipt Details
Date 30/09/2017
Amount 111.60
Reference

Show All   From 13/01/2018   To 13/01/2018

Analysis Total 111.60

Save   Discard   Pay in Full   Wizard   Automatic   Dept.   Close

Step Three

Click on **Save** to record the payment on the account.

The balance on the **Bank Current Account** should now be **£2900.40** which is the original balance of £2668.80 plus the two receipts from customers, £120.00 and £111.60 .

Tools Favourites WebLinks News Feeds Help
Bank Accounts

New Record Reconcile Payment Supplier Remittance Receipt Customer Transfer Recurring Cash Flow Statement Reports

A/C	Name	Balance
1200	Bank Current Account	2900.40
1210	Bank Deposit Account	0.00
1220	Building Society Account	0.00
1230	Cash Account	252.00
1235	Cash Register	0.00
1240	Company Credit Card	0.00
1250	Credit Card Receipts	0.00

2 Credit payments

2.1 Paying suppliers

We can now look at the other common area for payments which is paying suppliers when the business has previously bought goods on credit. This is especially common for buying inventory/stock.

📖 Case study activity 27

Matt e-mails Chrissie and confirms that TotalPhoto Ltd can pay two outstanding suppliers on 30th September, as follows:

A 'payments to suppliers listing' shows details of the two payments Matt has authorised Chrissie to make.

Date	Receipt type	Customer	Amount (£)	Details
30/09/17	Cheque No 3567	MacKay Films Ltd	250.50	Payment of Invoice 1341
30/09/17	BACS transfer	The Stationery Cupboard	94.70 _94.68_	Payment of Invoices 209 and 216 and Credit Note 134C

Chrissie must now enter these supplier payments onto Sage.

(Step by step guidance follows on how to complete this task on the computerised accounting system).

Step One

Click the on the **Bank** module, make sure it is the **Bank Current Account** that is highlighted and then select **Supplier** from the menu at the top of the screen.

This screen will appear.

Step Two

Use the drop down menu to select the first supplier to pay (**MacKay Films Ltd**).

Enter the correct date and the cheque number **'3567'** in the Cheque No box.

Step Three

You can now enter the payment of **£250.50** in the payment column or select Pay in Full

Click on the **Save** button to ensure Sage posts the transaction to the correct accounts within the system.

Now enter the payment to The Stationery Cupboard.

Once you have done this, go back to your **Supplier** screen and check the outstanding balances.

The bank balance should now be **£2555.22** and your **Bank** screen should look like this:

📖 **Case study**

Chrissie now feels confident with posting credit customer receipts and credit supplier payments.

She is however aware that some of TotalPhoto Ltd's daily transactions are cash payments and receipts and therefore still needs to understand how these are processed.

Bank receipts and payments

8

Introduction

This chapter looks at a further group of common business transactions, addressing the processing of payments and receipts through the bank account.

In the AAT Access Award in Accounting Software assessment you will be tested on recording receipts and payments from a bank statement using computerised accounting software. You should also know how to process and record cash transactions accurately within the accounts.

KNOWLEDGE	CONTENTS
Record bank and cash transactions	1 Bank transactions
3.2 Record transactions from a bank statement	2 Cash transactions
3.3 Record cash transactions	

1 Bank transactions

1.1 Case study: an introduction

> 📖 **Case study**
>
> TotalPhoto Ltd have now received their bank statement and Chrissie has been asked to process the bank receipts and payments using the Sage software.
>
> Matt and Stuart have also made some cash sales and have paid for business related items using cash. They have given Chrissie the details and have asked her to process them as required within Sage.
>
> You should complete the activities throughout his chapter as if you were Chrissie.

1.2 Common payments and receipts

Businesses deal with a wide range of monetary transactions every day of the week.

These include money being paid to the business from customers (receipts) and money being paid by the business to others (payments). In the last chapter we looked at how to process receipts from credit customers and payments to credit suppliers.

The income and expenditure of a business also includes other types of payments and receipts, below are a few examples:

Receipts

- Receipts from cash customers for goods bought by cash/cheque/credit card

- Receipts from customers for goods/services sold on credit

- Other receipts such as: money received from the sales of a fixed asset i.e. a motor vehicle, interest received from the bank, rent received from tenants who rent rooms in your premises.

Payments

- Payments made to suppliers (for goods/services bought on credit)

- Payments made to meet other expenses i.e. bills such as gas, electric etc.

- Payment of salaries and wages to staff

1.3   Sage bank accounts

To record this, Sage allows you to run a number of 'bank accounts'. These need not necessarily all be held at a Bank Current Account – they could also include cash in hand and recorded in the Cash Account.

The principles for making payments in or out of any of these accounts are the same.

Enter the **Bank** module. You can see that Sage has already set up a number of different bank accounts, each with its own Nominal Code. You can of course amend these or add to them if you wish. In this particular example, the **Cash Account** is nominal code **1230**, the **Bank Current Account** will always be nominal code **1200**.

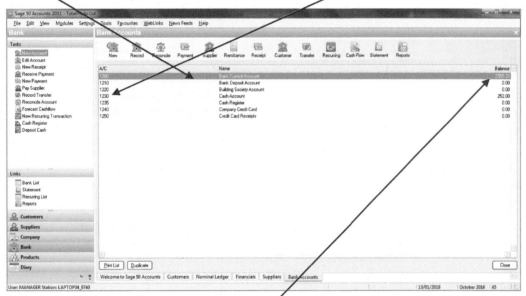

The most commonly used bank account is Nominal Code 1200 (Bank Current Account).

This is the one that you will use in this manual for payments in and out of TotalPhoto Ltd's main current account. You can see that it has a balance at the moment of **£2,555.22**.

You can view the transactions that have already been processed in this account by double-clicking on the **Bank Account**.

From this screen you need to select the **Activity** tab at the top.

Here you can see that the balance of the Bank Current Account is made up of:

Opening balance	£668.80
Additional Capital Introduced	£2,000.00
The receipt from Lullabies	£120.00
The receipt from Mrs H Poppy	£111.60
The payment to Mackay Films Ltd.	(£250.50)
The payment to The Stationery Cupboard	(£94.68)
Balance of Bank Current Account	£2,555.22

1.4 Recording receipts from cash customers

Cash sales are transactions that relate to sales made for cash rather than on credit. The funds are received immediately by the business in the form of cheque or card.

📖 Case study activity 28

TotalPhoto Ltd also sells items to two customers who pay by debit card on 30th September.

The first of these is a 6" × 4" Colour Print for £12.00 plus VAT (use nominal code 4000); the second is for School Photos (Set 2) for £28.00 plus VAT of 20% (nominal code 4003).

Chrissie is asked to enter these cash sales into the bank current account on Sage.

(Step by step guidance follows on how to complete this task on the computerised accounting system).

Step One

Select the **Bank module** and make sure that the **Bank Current Account** is highlighted. Click on the **Receipt** button.

Step Two

Enter each transaction on a separate line. Be careful to make sure you select the appropriate nominal code for each sale, and also the correct VAT rate. (T1 for standard or T9 for exempt).

Your entries should look like this:

Step Three

Click the **SAVE** button to post your entries to Sage.

Case study activity 29

Stuart at TotalPhoto Ltd also buys two items and pays via cheque on 30th September.

The first of these is 2 packs of specialist photo paper for £34.00 (nominal code 5001); the second is for stationery at a cost of £56.50 plus VAT of 20% (nominal code 5003).

Chrissie needs to enter these payments into the bank current account on Sage.

(Step by step guidance follows on how to complete this task on the computerised accounting system).

Step One

Select the Bank module and make sure that the **Bank Current Account** is highlighted. Click on the **Payment** button.

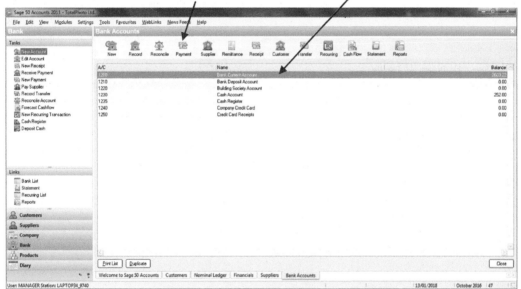

Step Two

Enter each transaction on a separate line. Be careful to make sure you select the appropriate nominal code for each purchase, and also the correct VAT rate. (T1 for standard or T9 for exempt).

Your entries should look like this:

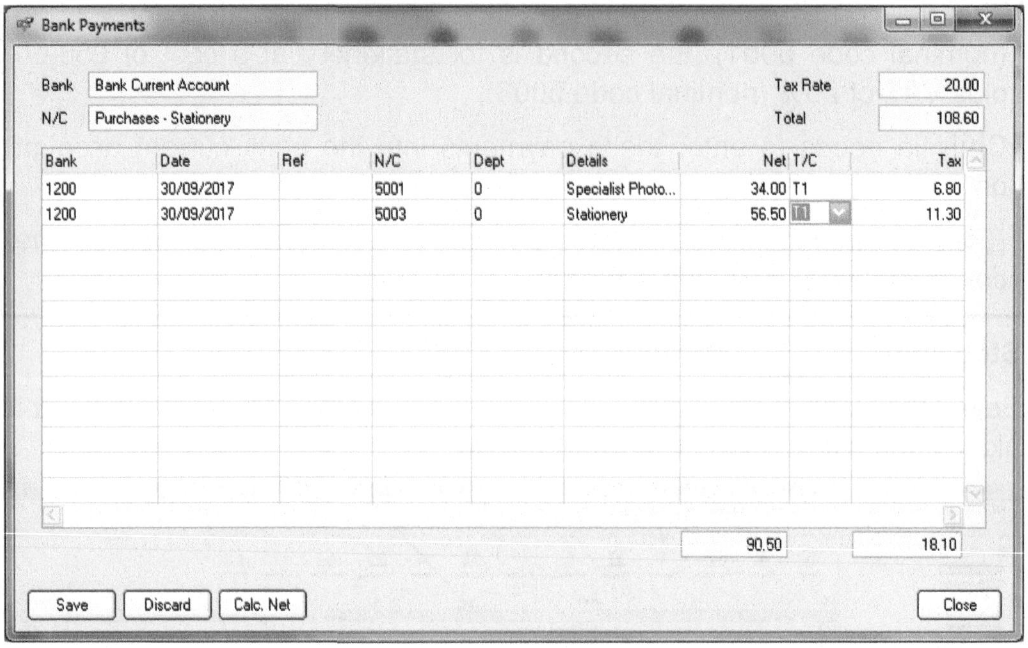

Step Three

Click the **SAVE** button to post your entries to Sage.

> ### 📖✏️ Case study activity 30
>
> TotalPhoto Ltd have received a bank statement, but the following transactions within the bank statement have not been entered onto the system. Chrissie has been asked to process the payments and receipts into Sage.
>
> She should take extra care to ensure that the correct nominal codes are used for each transaction.
>
> | ABS Bank |
> | --- |
>
> ABS Bank
> 141 High Street
> London
> WC17 4NQ
>
> TotalPhoto Ltd.
> Unit 63 Bailey Industrial Estate
> Fornby Road
> Miltonby
> Lancashire
> LD37 7QZ
>
> Statement Date: 30th September 2017
>
> Statement Number: 102
>
> Account Number: 12345678
>
> Sort Code: 11-22-33
>
> | Date | Details | Debit | Credit | Balance |
> | --- | --- | --- | --- | --- |
> | 30th Sep | Opening Balance | | | 2494.62 |
> | 30th Sep | Debit Card – Sale School photo * | | 15.00 | 2509.62 |
> | 30th Sep | Wages | 345.60 | | 2164.02 |
> | 30th Sep | Telephone * | 45.45 | | 2118.57 |
> | 30th Sep | Chq – Sale Corporate * | | 225.00 | 2343.57 |
> | 30th Sep | Advertising * | 100.00 | | 2243.57 |
> | 30th Sep | Gas * | 54.40 | | 2189.17 |
> | 30th Sep | Electric * | 32.00 | | 2157.17 |
>
> **Note:** The transactions above that are marked with a * above are subject to VAT. As the amount shown is the amount *actually* paid out or paid in, these amounts are **inclusive of VAT** and should be entered accordingly.
>
> *(Guidance on how to process the receipts follows).*

Step one

To enter the receipts, select **Receipt** from the bank module.

Step two

Enter the receipts from the bank statement. **Remember,** the amounts shown are inclusive of VAT and therefore you will need to enter the full amount and then click the **Calc Net** button.

Your screen should look like this:

Step Three

Click the **SAVE** button to post your entries to Sage.

📖✏️ Case study activity 31

Chrissie now needs to post the payments from the bank statement.

She remembers from her training that she needs to take particular care when selecting the nominal accounts and when dealing with VAT.

ABS Bank
141 High Street
London
WC17 4NQ

TotalPhoto Ltd.
Unit 63 Bailey Industrial Estate
Fornby Road
Miltonby
Lancashire
LD37 7QZ

Statement Date: 30th September 2017

Statement Number: 102

Account Number: 12345678

Sort Code: 11-22-33

Date	Details	Debit	Credit	Balance
30th Sep	Opening Balance			2494.62
30th Sep	Debit Card – Sale School photo *		15.00	2509.62
30th Sep	Wages	345.60		2164.02
30th Sep	Telephone *	45.45		2118.57
30th Sep	Chq – Sale Corporate *		225.00	2343.57
30th Sep	Advertising *	100.00		2243.57
30th Sep	Gas *	54.40		2189.17
30th Sep	Electric *	32.00		2157.17

Remember! The transactions above that are marked with a * above are subject to VAT. As the amount shown is the amount *actually* paid out or paid in, these amounts are **inclusive of VAT** you should use the **Calc Net** button when posting.

When you have finished entering the payments onto Sage, your screen should look like this:

Click **SAVE** to post your transactions to Sage.

Once you have posted all of the Bank transactions, you should be able to check that you have done everything correctly because the balance on your **Bank Current Account** on Sage should match the balance on the bank statement given above.

2 Cash transactions

2.1 Cash payments and receipts

Cash payments and receipts are recorded in exactly the same way as any other payments made from a bank account. The only difference is that you need to make sure that the **Cash Account** is highlighted in the Bank module before posting anything.

Also be sure to enter the correct VAT code for each transaction. Many items commonly paid for out of cash are zero-rated or exempt – but not all.

For standard rated items you use the tax code (T/C) T1

For zero-rated items you will use the tax code (T/C) T0

For exempt items you will use the tax code (T/C) T9

You will be using the Cash Account (1230) for all cash payment and receipt transactions.

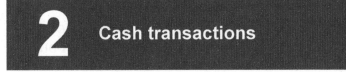 **Case study activity 32**

The directors of TotalPhoto Ltd make the following payments out of cash on 30th September 2017.

Voucher No	Description	Amount	VAT?
11762	Window cleaner	£4.00	No
11763	Tea and milk	£2.65	No
11764	Magazine subscription	£3.00	No
11765	Stamps	£3.60	No
11766	Pens	£1.99	Inclusive at 20.0%
11767	Taxi fare	£8.00	Inclusive at 20.0%

Chrissie is given the details of these payments and asked to enter them on to Sage.

(Step by step guidance follows on how to complete this task on the computerised accounting system).

Step One

Select the Bank module and make sure that the **Cash** Account is highlighted. Enter the above payments by clicking on the **Payment** button.

Step Two

Enter each of the transactions above the same way as you did for the bank payments.

Your screen should look like this:

Bank Payments								
Bank	Cash Account					Tax Rate		20.00
N/C	Travelling					Total		23.24
Bank	Date	Ref	N/C	Dept	Details	Net	T/C	Tax
1230	30/09/2017	11762	7801	0	Window Cleaner	4.00	T0	0.00
1230	30/09/2017	11763	8205	0	Tea and milk	2.65	T0	0.00
1230	30/09/2017	11764	8201	0	Magazine Subs...	3.00	T0	0.00
1230	30/09/2017	11765	7501	0	Stamps	3.60	T0	0.00
1230	30/09/2017	11766	7504	0	Pens	1.66	T1	0.33
1230	30/09/2017	11767	7400	0	Taxi Fare	6.67	T1	1.33
						21.58		1.66

Save   Discard   Calc. Net   Close

Step Three

Once you have verified this click **SAVE**.

📖 Case study activity 33

TotalPhoto Ltd have made a number of sales where the customer paid cash.

Chrissie now needs to enter the following cash receipts into the Cash Account on Sage. All amounts shown are inclusive of VAT.

Description	Amount
Family photo	£24.00
Individual photo	£14.00
Nursery Photos	£21.00
Corporate photos	£85.00
School photos	£21.00

Your screen should look like this:

Once you have verified this click **Save.**

Case study activity 34

To check that everything has been entered correctly, Chrissie should produce a revised Trial Balance.

The Trial Balance should now look like this:

Date:	16/01/2018		TotalPhoto Ltd.		Page:	1
Time:	13:39:19		**Period Trial Balance**			

To Period: Month 12, September 2017

N/C	Name	Debit	Credit
1100	Debtors Control Account	112.20	
1200	Bank Current Account	2,157.17	
1230	Cash Account	393.76	
2100	Creditors Control Account		566.12
2200	VAT on Sales		502.16
2201	VAT on Purchases	592.84	
3000	Capital		3,000.00
4000	Sales - Individuals and Family		645.97
4001	Sales - Weddings		433.50
4002	Sales - Corporate		1,255.83
4003	Sales - Nurseries & Schools		175.50
5000	Purchases - Film	1,777.65	
5001	Purchases - Paper	196.52	
5002	Purchases - Cartridges & Toner	309.25	
5003	Purchases - Stationery	479.30	
6201	Advertising	83.33	
7004	Wages - Regular	345.60	
7200	Electricity	26.67	
7201	Gas	45.33	
7400	Travelling	6.67	
7501	Postage and Carriage	3.60	
7502	Telephone	37.88	
7504	Office Stationery	1.66	
7801	Cleaning	4.00	
8201	Subscriptions	3.00	
8205	Refreshments	2.65	
	Totals:	6,579.08	6,579.08

Reports using accounting software

9

Introduction

This chapter looks at the reporting process within Sage.

Reporting forms a very important part of the day to day running of an accounts department. Within the AAT assessment, you will be asked to generate specific reports and upload them in PDF format to the examination software. The process of how you can do this is detailed within this chapter and you should pay particular attention to this.

You should take time to familiarise yourself with the reports section of the software and make note of what information is detailed within each report.

KNOWLEDGE
Produce reports using accounting software
4.1 Reports that may be produced using accounting software
4.2 Produce reports using accounting software

CONTENTS
1   Customer reports
2   Supplier reports
3   Nominal ledger reports
4   Bank and cash reports

1 Customer reports

1.1 Case study: an introduction

> ### 📖 Case study
>
> As it is month end, Matt and Stuart at TotalPhoto would like to assess the success of the new accounting software and review some of the transactions for the month of September.
>
> They are particularly interested in the different types of reports that can be created using Sage and have asked Chrissie to produce a number of them to review at the month-end meeting at the end of the week.
>
> You should complete the activities throughout his chapter as if you were Chrissie.

1.2 Computerised accounting reports

Although it is possible to create and produce your own Sage reports, there are a number of extremely useful report layouts already set up within Sage. You have already seen a number of these as we have been working through this book.

You should now make yourself familiar with these, plus the other reports shown below.

Note: There are many other reports within Sage; you should take the time to examine all of these to find the reports that will best suit your business. For the purpose of the AAT assessment, you will be required to produce specific reports using Sage and then you will upload these to the examination platform so they can be marked by AAT. In order to do this, you will be required to export each report to PDF format and save it. You will then upload all of the reports that you have produced at the end of the assessment. The steps you need to follow in order to export reports to PDF are shown below.

Have a go at practising generating reports using the **Reports** icon within each module. Look at the details contained within each report and familiarise yourself with them. This will form an important part of your assessment.

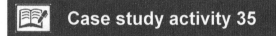

Case study activity 35

Chrissie should start by producing customer and supplier activity reports.

1.3   Customer Activity Report

The Customer Activity Report can be accessed as follows:

Customers – Reports – Customer Activity Reports – Customer Activity

The Customer Activity Report shows all transactions for a single, or range of, customers, including sales, returns and invoices.

To generate this report you need to select the **Customers** module and then the **Reports** icon.

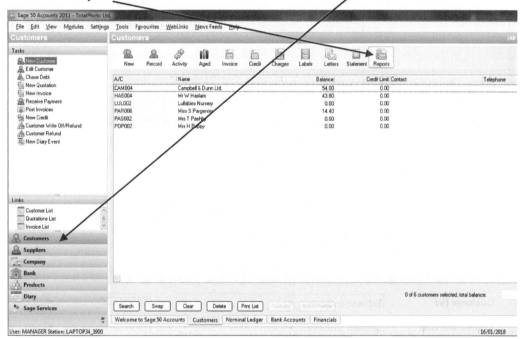

From this screen, you select **Customer Activity Reports** and then select which customer activity report you wish to use. For the purpose of this activity we will use the detailed report. In the AAT assessment it does not matter which one you select unless it specifically states which one to use.

Double-click on the report name. We don't have any specified details to add into this screen for this activity. If the assessment gave you a specific date range for example, you would enter that here. Once you are happy, click **next.**

Your report should look like this:

Date:	16/01/2018				**TotalPhoto Ltd.**					Page:	1
Time:	14:24:21				**Customer Activity (Detailed)**						

Date From:	01/01/1980			Customer From:	
Date To:	16/01/2018			Customer To:	ZZZZZZZZ
Transaction From:	1			N/C From:	
Transaction To:	99,999,999			N/C To:	99999999
Inc b/fwd transaction:	No			Dept From:	0
Exc later payment:	No			Dept To:	999

** NOTE: All report values are shown in Base Currency, unless otherwise indicated **

A/C:	CAM004	Name:	Campbell & Dunn Ltd.		Contact:					Tel:		

No	Type	Date	Ref	N/C	Details	Dept	T/C	Value	O/S	Debit	Credit	V	B
33	SI	30/09/2017	4895	4002	Corporate	0	T1	54.00 *	54.00	54.00		N	-
						Totals:		54.00	54.00	54.00			

Amount Outstanding	54.00
Amount Paid this period	0.00
Credit Limit £	0.00
Turnover YTD	45.00

A/C:	HAS004	Name:	Mr W Haslam		Contact:					Tel:		

No	Type	Date	Ref	N/C	Details	Dept	T/C	Value	O/S	Debit	Credit	V	B
30	SI	30/09/2017	4892	4000	Individuals and Family	0	T1	29.40 *	29.40	29.40		N	-
34	SI	30/09/2017	4896	4000	Individuals and Family	0	T1	14.40 *	14.40	14.40		N	-
						Totals:		43.80	43.80	43.80			

Amount Outstanding	43.80
Amount Paid this period	0.00
Credit Limit £	0.00
Turnover YTD	36.50

A/C:	LUL002	Name:	Lullabies Nursery		Contact:					Tel:		

No	Type	Date	Ref	N/C	Details	Dept	T/C	Value	O/S	Debit	Credit	V	B
32	SI	30/09/2017	4894	4003	Nursery	0	T1	120.00		120.00		N	-
42	SR	30/09/2017	Cheque	1200	Sales Receipt	0	T9	120.00			120.00	-	N

To export this to PDF format ready for upload, click on **Export** from the menu at the top.

Preview
Open Export Print Page Setup Printer Offsets Email Zoom In Zoom Out Close Goto Page |1|

Date:	16/01/2018			**TotalPhoto Ltd.**
Time:	14:24:21			**Customer Activity (Detailed)**

Date From:	01/01/1980
Date To:	16/01/2018
Transaction From:	1
Transaction To:	99,999,999
Inc b/fwd transaction:	No
Exc later payment:	No

** NOTE: All report values are shown in Base Currency, unless oth

From this screen, select a suitable location to save your work, save it using the name/format stated in the AAT assessment. For the purpose of this activity we will call it 'Customer Activity'. From the dropdown menu, select **PDF** as the format.

When you click **save** this report will be saved in the correct format. Exporting information to spreadsheet format is exactly the same process, you simply select 'Excel' from the format dropdown instead of PDF.

Note: It is extremely important that you practice exporting your reports to PDF format as this is how they will need to be produced in your live assessment. These will need to be uploaded in the assessment, failure to do this will mean that your work cannot be seen and marked by AAT and this would result in a Not Yet Competent result.

1.4 Customer Address List

The Customer Address List can be viewed as follows:

Customers – Reports – Customer Details Reports – Customer Address List

The Customer Address List report shows contact details for customers, including addresses, contact names, telephone numbers and fax numbers.

Date: 16/01/2018	TotalPhoto Ltd.		Page: 1
Time: 14:38:07	**Customer Address List**		

Customer From:
Customer To: ZZZZZZZZ

A/C	Name & Address	Contact Name	Telephone	Fax
CAM004	Campbell & Dunn Ltd. 12 The Beeches Miltonby Lancashire LN87 9PP			
HAS004	Mr W Haslam 22 Brown Street Miltonby Lancashire LN87 6FD			
LUL002	Lullabies Nursery 104 Victoria Road Miltonby Lancashire LN87 5PS			
PAR006	Miss S Pargenter 11 Alexandra Park Miltonby Lancashire LN87 2WD			
PAS002	Mrs T Pashby 30A Andrews Street Killington Lancashire LN85 6TT			
POP002	Mrs H Poppy 120 Forrest Way Miltonby			

1.5 The Sales Day Book

The Sales Day Book report can be generated as follows:

Customers – Reports – Day Book Reports – Day Books: Customer Invoices

The sales day book shows details of all of the sales invoices that have been inputted into the system for a certain date range (specified by you), and to which customer account code they have been posted.

Date:	16/01/2018						TotalPhoto Ltd.					Page:	1
Time:	16:34:30						Day Books: Customer Invoices (Detailed)						

| Date From: | 01/01/1980 | | | | | | | | | Customer From: | | | |
| Date To: | 31/12/2019 | | | | | | | | | Customer To: | | ZZZZZZZZ | |

| Transaction From: | 1 | | | | | | | | | N/C From: | | | |
| Transaction To: | 99,999,999 | | | | | | | | | N/C To: | | 99999999 | |

| Dept From: | 0 | | | | | | | | | | | | |
| Dept To: | 999 | | | | | | | | | | | | |

Tran No.	Type	Date	A/C Ref	N/C	Inv Ref	Dept.	Details	Net Amount	Tax Amount	T/C	Gross Amount	V	B
29	SI	30/09/2017	POP002	4001	4891	0	Wedding	105.00	21.00	T1	126.00	N	-
30	SI	30/09/2017	HAS004	4000	4892	0	Individuals and Family	24.50	4.90	T1	29.40	N	-
31	SI	30/09/2017	PAR006	4000	4893	0	Individuals and Family	12.00	2.40	T1	14.40	N	-
32	SI	30/09/2017	LUL002	4003	4894	0	Nursery	100.00	20.00	T1	120.00	N	-
33	SI	30/09/2017	CAM004	4002	4895	0	Corporate	45.00	9.00	T1	54.00	N	-
34	SI	30/09/2017	HAS004	4000	4896	0	Individuals and Family	12.00	2.40	T1	14.40	N	-
							Totals:	298.50	59.70		358.20		

1.6 The Sales Returns Day Book

The Sales Returns Day Book is accessed in a similar way:

Customers – Reports – Day Book Reports – Day Books: Customer Credits

The sales returns day book shows details of all of the sales credit notes that have been inputted into the system for a certain date range (specified by you), and to which customer account code they have been posted.

Date:	16/01/2018						TotalPhoto Ltd.					Page:	1
Time:	16:37:00						Day Books: Customer Credits (Detailed)						

| Date From: | 01/01/1980 | | | | | | | | | Customer From: | | | |
| Date To: | 31/12/2019 | | | | | | | | | Customer To: | | ZZZZZZZZ | |

| Transaction From: | 1 | | | | | | | | | N/C From: | | | |
| Transaction To: | 99,999,999 | | | | | | | | | N/C To: | | 99999999 | |

| Dept From: | 0 | | | | | | | | | | | | |
| Dept To: | 999 | | | | | | | | | | | | |

Tran No.	Type	Date	A/C Ref	N/C	Inv Ref	Dept.	Details	Net Amount	Tax Amount	T/C	Gross Amount	V	B
35	SC	30/09/2017	POP002	4000	25	0	Return of colour print	12.00	2.40	T1	14.40	N	-
							Totals:	12.00	2.40		14.40		

1.7 The Aged Debtor Analysis

The Aged Debtor's Analysis report can be found as follows:

Customers – Reports – Aged Debtor's Reports – Aged Debtor's Analysis

The Aged Debtor's (sometimes called the Aged Receivables) analysis shows details of any monies outstanding from credit customers. Italso breaks the debts down into timescales of 30, 60, 90 and 90+ days so that you can see how old any particular debt is which helps with knowing which are a priority to chase for payment.

Date: 16/01/2018			TotalPhoto Ltd.					Page: 1	
Time: 16:40:35			**Aged Debtors Analysis (Detailed)**						

Date From:	01/01/1980					Customer From:		
Date To:	16/01/2018					Customer To:	ZZZZZZZ	
Include future transactions:	No							
Exclude later payments:	No							

** NOTE: All report values are shown in Base Currency, unless otherwise indicated **

A/C: CAM004	Name:	Campbell & Dunn Ltd.		Contact:				Tel:		

No	Type	Date	Ref	Details	Balance	Future	Current	Period 1	Period 2	Period 3	Older
33	SI	30/09/2017	4895	Corporate	54.00	0.00	0.00	0.00	0.00	54.00	0.00
				Totals:	54.00	0.00	0.00	0.00	0.00	54.00	0.00

Turnover:	45.00
Credit Limit £	0.00

A/C: HAS004	Name:	Mr W Haslam		Contact:				Tel:		

No	Type	Date	Ref	Details	Balance	Future	Current	Period 1	Period 2	Period 3	Older
30	SI	30/09/2017	4892	Individuals and Family	29.40	0.00	0.00	0.00	0.00	29.40	0.00
34	SI	30/09/2017	4896	Individuals and Family	14.40	0.00	0.00	0.00	0.00	14.40	0.00
				Totals:	43.80	0.00	0.00	0.00	0.00	43.80	0.00

Turnover:	36.50
Credit Limit £	0.00

A/C: PAR006	Name:	Miss S Pargenter		Contact:				Tel:		

No	Type	Date	Ref	Details	Balance	Future	Current	Period 1	Period 2	Period 3	Older
31	SI	30/09/2017	4893	Individuals and Family	14.40	0.00	0.00	0.00	0.00	14.40	0.00
				Totals:	14.40	0.00	0.00	0.00	0.00	14.40	0.00

Turnover:	12.00
Credit Limit £	0.00

				Grand Totals:	112.20	0.00	0.00	0.00	0.00	112.20	0.00

2 Supplier reports

2.1 Supplier Activity Report

The Supplier Activity Report is accessed using the following:

Suppliers – Reports – Supplier Activity Reports – Supplier Activity

The Supplier Activity Report shows all transactions for a single, or range of, suppliers, including purchases, returns and invoices.

Date: 16/01/2018				**TotalPhoto Ltd.**					Page: 1		
Time: 16:54:52				**Supplier Activity (Detailed)**							

Date From:	01/01/1980						Supplier From:	
Date To:	16/01/2018						Supplier To:	ZZZZZZZZ
Transaction From:	1						N/C From:	
Transaction To:	99,999,999						N/C To:	99999999
Inc b/fwd transaction:	No						Dept From:	0
Exc later payment:	No						Dept To:	999

** NOTE: All report values are shown in Base Currency, unless otherwise indicated **

A/C:	MF001	Name:	Mackay Films Ltd.			Contact:	Carl Richardson			Tel:	01828 827493		
No	Type	Date	Ref	N/C	Details		Dept	T/C	Value	O/S	Debit	Credit	V B
36	PI	30/09/2017	1341	5000	Film		0	T1	250.50	0.00		250.50	N
44	PP	30/09/2017	3567	1200	Purchase Payment		0	T9	250.50	0.00	250.50		N
						Totals:			0.00	0.00	250.50	250.50	

Amount Outstanding	0.00
Amount paid this period	250.50
Credit Limit £	0.00
Turnover YTD	208.75

A/C:	MP002	Name:	Mills Paper Products			Contact:	Mr Shaun Square			Tel:	07126 378918		
No	Type	Date	Ref	N/C	Details		Dept	T/C	Value	O/S	Debit	Credit	V B
40	PI	30/09/2017	10092	5001	Paper		0	T1	195.02 *	195.02		195.02	N
						Totals:			195.02	195.02	0.00	195.02	

Amount Outstanding	195.02

2.2 Supplier Address List

The **Supplier Address List** report can be viewed as follows:

Suppliers – Reports – Supplier Details Reports – Supplier Address List

The Supplier Address List report shows contact details for suppliers, including addresses, contact names, telephone numbers and fax numbers.

Date: 16/01/2018		TotalPhoto Ltd.		Page: 1
Time: 16:59:19		**Supplier Address List**		

Supplier From:
Supplier To: ZZZZZZZZ

A/C	Name	Contact	Telephone	Fax
AP004	Arthur's Photographic Equipment Ltd. 77 Overton Lane Birmingham BM97 8YK	Jennie Reeves	0121 299 0192	
KF001	K2 Films Ltd. Tokyo House 72 - 84 Great Milne Street London WC4 6DD	Kim Nakajima	0207 867 6599	
MF001	Mackay Films Ltd. 33 West Parade Miltonby Lancashire LN87 7HD	Carl Richardson	01828 827493	
MP002	Mills Paper Products 405 Ream Road Bradford West Yorkshire BD5 6QA	Mr Shaun Squire	07126 378918	

2.3 The Purchases Day Book

Similar to the Sales Day Book, but for transactions made with suppliers, **The Purchases Day Book** report is accessed using the following:

Suppliers – Reports – Day Book Reports – Day Books: Supplier Invoices

The purchases day book shows details of all of the purchases invoices that have been inputted into the system for a certain date range (specified by you), and to which supplier account code they have been posted.

Date: 16/01/2018		TotalPhoto Ltd.		Page: 1
Time: 17:05:56		**Day Books: Supplier Invoices (Detailed)**		

| Date From: | 01/01/1980 | | | Supplier From: | |
| Date To: | 31/12/2019 | | | Supplier To: | ZZZZZZZZ |

Transaction From: 1
Transaction To: 99,999,999

N/C From:
N/C To: 99999999

Dept From: 0
Dept To: 999

Tran No.	Type	Date	A/C Ref	N/C	Inv Ref	Dept	Details	Net Amount	Tax Amount	T/C	Gross Amount	V	B
36	PI	30/09/2017	MF001	5000	1341	0	Film	208.75	41.75	T1	250.50	N	-
37	PI	30/09/2017	SC003	5003	209	0	Stationery	14.65	2.93	T1	17.58	N	-
38	PI	30/09/2017	SC003	5003	216	0	Stationery	78.90	15.78	T1	94.68	N	-
39	PI	30/09/2017	O1001	5002	2203	0	Cartridges & Toners	309.25	61.85	T1	371.10	N	-
40	PI	30/09/2017	MP002	5001	10092	0	Paper	162.52	32.50	T1	195.02	N	-
							Totals	774.07	154.81		928.88		

2.4 The Purchases Returns Day Book

The Purchases Returns Day Book report can be run as follows:

Suppliers – Reports – Day Book Reports – Day Books: Supplier Credits

The purchases returns day book shows details of all of the purchase credit notes that have been inputted into the system for a certain date range (specified by you), and to which supplier account code they have been posted.

Date: 16/01/2018						TotalPhoto Ltd.			Page: 1			
Time: 17:07:40						Day Books: Supplier Credits (Detailed)						
Date From:		01/01/1980							Supplier From:			
Date To:		31/12/2019							Supplier To:		ZZZZZZZZ	
Transaction From:		1							N/C From:			
Transaction To:		99,999,999							N/C To:		99999999	
Dept From:		0										
Dept To:		999										
Tran No.	Type	Date	A/C Ref	N/C	Inv Ref	Dept	Details	Net Amount	Tax Amount	T/C	Gross Amount	V B
41	PC	30/09/2017	SC003	5003	134C	0	Incorrect goods supplied	14.65	2.93	T1	17.58	N -
							Totals	14.65	2.93		17.58	

2.5 The Aged Creditor's Analysis

The Aged Creditor's Analysis can be viewed using the following:

Suppliers – Reports – Aged Creditor's Reports – Aged Creditor's Analysis

The Aged Creditor's (sometimes called the Aged Payables) analysis shows details of any monies owed to credit suppliers. It breaks the outstanding amounts down into timescales of 30, 60, 90 and 90+ days so that you can see how old any particular debt is and who to make a priority for payment.

This report is shown on the following page.

Date: 16/01/2018				TotalPhoto Ltd.					Page: 1	
Time: 17:12:26				**Aged Creditors Analysis (Detailed)**						

| Date From: | 01/01/1980 | | | | | | Supplier From: | | | |
| Date To: | 16/01/2018 | | | | | | Supplier To: | ZZZZZZZZ | | |

Include future transactions: No
Exclude later payments: No

** NOTE: All report values are shown in Base Currency, unless otherwise indicated **

A/C:	MP002	Name:	Mills Paper Products		Contact:	Mr Shaun Square		Tel:	07126 378918	
No:	**Type**	**Date**	**Ref**	**Details**	**Balance**	**Future**	**Current**	**Period 1**	**Period 2**	**Period 3**	**Older**
40	PI	30/09/2017	10092	Paper	195.02	0.00	0.00	0.00	0.00	195.02	0.00
				Totals:	195.02	0.00	0.00	0.00	0.00	195.02	0.00

Turnover: 162.52
Credit Limit £ 0.00

A/C:	OI001	Name:	Octopus Inks Ltd		Contact:	Sheila Cribbley		Tel:	0191 252 4132	
No:	**Type**	**Date**	**Ref**	**Details**	**Balance**	**Future**	**Current**	**Period 1**	**Period 2**	**Period 3**	**Older**
39	PI	30/09/2017	2203	Cartridges & Toners	371.10	0.00	0.00	0.00	0.00	371.10	0.00
				Totals:	371.10	0.00	0.00	0.00	0.00	371.10	0.00

Turnover: 309.25
Credit Limit £ 0.00

			Grand Totals:	566.12	0.00	0.00	0.00	0.00	566.12	0.00

3 Nominal ledger reports

3.1 Nominal ledger reports

There are a number of nominal ledger reports available. To access these, select the **Company** module and then **Reports.**

You should familiarise yourself with the contents of this section and explore in more detail what each of the reports are showing. Below are some that you may find useful when preparing for your AAT assessment.

3.2 The Nominal Activity Report

The Nominal Activity Report can be accessed using the following steps:

Company – Reports – Nominal Activity Reports – Nominal Activity (excluding no transactions)

This report will generate a copy of each account within your nominal ledger which has transactions within it. It is useful to print the 'excluding no transactions' report otherwise you will end up producing a report with every single account on it, even if there is nothing in the account. Your report should look like this.

Date:	16/01/2018			**TotalPhoto Ltd.**					Page:	1		
Time:	18:54:53			**Nominal Activity - Excluding No Transactions**								
Date From:	01/01/1980							N/C From:				
Date To:	16/01/2018							N/C To:	99999999			
Transaction From:	1											
Transaction To:	99,999,999											

N/C:	1100		Name:	Debtors Control Account					Account Balance:		112.20 DR		
No	**Type**	**Date**	**Account**	**Ref**	**Details**	**Dept**	**T/C**	**Value**	**Debit**	**Credit**	**V**	**B**
29	SI	30/09/2017	POP002	4891	Wedding	0	T1	126.00	126.00		N	-
30	SI	30/09/2017	HAS004	4892	Individuals and Family	0	T1	29.40	29.40		N	-
31	SI	30/09/2017	PAR006	4893	Individuals and Family	0	T1	14.40	14.40		N	-
32	SI	30/09/2017	LUL002	4894	Nursery	0	T1	120.00	120.00		N	-
33	SI	30/09/2017	CAM004	4895	Corporate	0	T1	54.00	54.00		N	-
34	SI	30/09/2017	HAS004	4896	Individuals and Family	0	T1	14.40	14.40		N	-
35	SC	30/09/2017	POP002	25	Return of colour print	0	T1	14.40		14.40	N	-
42	SR	30/09/2017	LUL002	Cheque	Sales Receipt	0	T9	120.00		120.00	-	N
43	SR	30/09/2017	POP002		Sales Receipt	0	T9	111.60		111.60	-	N
							Totals:		358.20	246.00		
							History Balance:		112.20			

N/C:	1200		Name:	Bank Current Account					Account Balance:		2,157.17 DR		
No	**Type**	**Date**	**Account**	**Ref**	**Details**	**Dept**	**T/C**	**Value**	**Debit**	**Credit**	**V**	**B**
1	JD	30/09/2017	1200	O/Bal	Opening Balance	0	T9	668.80	668.80		-	-
21	JD	15/09/2017	1200	J001	Capital introduced by Matt Evans	0	T9	2,000.00	2,000.00		-	N
42	SR	30/09/2017	LUL002	Cheque	Sales Receipt	0	T9	120.00	120.00		-	N
43	SR	30/09/2017	POP002		Sales Receipt	0	T9	111.60	111.60		-	N
44	PP	30/09/2017	MF001	3567	Purchase Payment	0	T9	250.50		250.50	-	N
45	PP	30/09/2017	SC003		Purchase Payment	0	T9	94.68		94.68	-	N
46	BR	30/09/2017	1200		Colour Print	0	T1	14.40	14.40		N	N
47	BR	30/09/2017	1200		School Photos (Set 2)	0	T1	33.60	33.60		N	N
48	BP	30/09/2017	1200		Specialist Photo Paper	0	T1	40.80		40.80	N	N
49	BP	30/09/2017	1200		Stationery	0	T1	67.80		67.80	N	N

Within the AAT assessment, you may be required to produce the details of just one of the accounts within the nominal ledger, for example, Sales – Nurseries & Schools. AAT will specify within the assessment which account it is that they want you to produce so it is no use producing the full nominal activity.

The following steps should be followed to produce the details of just one specified account, for the purpose of this task we will use Sales – Nurseries & Schools.

Step one

From the **Company** module, locate the **account** that you would like to run a report on and highlight it. (Make sure that no other accounts are highlighted as they too will be included in your report).

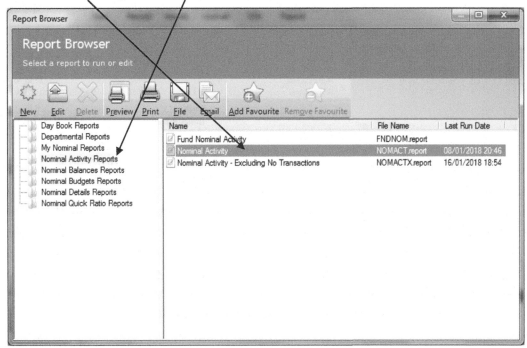

Step two

Click on reports, **Nominal Activity Reports** and then double-click on **Nominal Activity.**

Step three

Click **OK** when this screen appears (or specify the date range if required in the assessment)

Your report should look like this:

This report can be run for a few different accounts at the same time. To do this you simply highlight the ones that you require.

Once you have run the report, it is important to clear everything that you have highlighted, as all other reports that you run will only pick up information to do with those selected accounts.

To clear it off, you can either click back on the account where it is highlighted and this will un-highlight it. Alternatively, you can click **Clear** from the company module screen as shown on the following page.

3.3 The Trial Balance

The Trial Balance is a further report which can be run, as follows:

Company – Financials (in the links section) – Trial (on the menu at the top of the screen)

The trial balance shows a list of all account balances and whether they are a debit or credit balance.

Date:	16/01/2018	TotalPhoto Ltd.		Page: 1
Time:	19:16:59	**Period Trial Balance**		

To Period: Month 12, September 2017

N/C	Name	Debit	Credit
1100	Debtors Control Account	112.20	
1200	Bank Current Account	2,157.17	
1230	Cash Account	393.76	
2100	Creditors Control Account		566.12
2200	VAT on Sales		502.16
2201	VAT on Purchases	592.84	
3000	Capital		3,000.00
4000	Sales - Individuals and Family		645.97
4001	Sales - Weddings		433.50
4002	Sales - Corporate		1,255.83
4003	Sales - Nurseries & Schools		175.50
5000	Purchases - Film	1,777.65	
5001	Purchases - Paper	196.52	
5002	Purchases - Cartridges & Toner	309.25	
5003	Purchases - Stationery	479.30	
6201	Advertising	83.33	
7004	Wages - Regular	345.60	
7200	Electricity	26.67	
7201	Gas	45.33	
7400	Travelling	6.67	
7501	Postage and Carriage	3.60	
7502	Telephone	37.88	
7504	Office Stationery	1.66	
7801	Cleaning	4.00	
8201	Subscriptions	3.00	
8205	Refreshments	2.65	
	Totals:	**6,579.08**	**6,579.08**

3.4 The Statement of Profit and Loss

The Statement of Profit and Loss (Profit and Loss Account) can be accessed using the following:

Company – Financials (in the links section) – P and L (on the menu at the top of the screen)

The P and L report includes information on all of the income and expenses of a business, **it does not** include any information on the company's assets or liabilities. This report is one of the required financial statements at the end of an accounting year and is useful for making business decisions.

Date:	16/01/2018	TotalPhoto Ltd.		Page:	1
Time:	19:21:15	**Profit and Loss**			

From:	Month 1, October 2016			
To:	Month 12, September 2017			

Chart of Accounts:		Default Layout of Accounts			

	Period		Year to Date	
Sales				
Product Sales	2,510.80		2,510.80	
		2,510.80		2,510.80
Purchases				
Purchases	2,762.72		2,762.72	
		2,762.72		2,762.72
Direct Expenses				
Sales Promotion	83.33		83.33	
		83.33		83.33
Gross Profit/(Loss):		(335.25)		(335.25)
Overheads				
Gross Wages	345.60		345.60	
Heat, Light and Power	72.00		72.00	
Travelling and Entertainment	6.67		6.67	
Printing and Stationery	43.14		43.14	
Maintenance	4.00		4.00	
General Expenses	5.65		5.65	
		477.06		477.06
Net Profit/(Loss):		(812.31)		(812.31)

3.5 The Statement of Financial Position

The Statement of Financial Position (Balance Sheet) is another important report both for accounting and business planning. It is accessed using:

Company – Financials (in the links section) – Balance (on the menu at the top of the screen)

The Balance Sheet report includes information on all of the assets and liabilities of a business, **it does not** include any information on the company's income or expenses. This report is one of the required financial statements at the end of an accounting year.

Date: 16/01/2018	TotalPhoto Ltd.			Page: 1	
Time: 19:24:07	**Balance Sheet**				
From: Month 1, October 2016					
To: Month 12, September 2017					
Chart of Account:	Default Layout of Accounts				
	Period		**Year to Date**		
Fixed Assets					
		0.00			0.00
Current Assets					
Debtors	112.20		112.20		
Deposits and Cash	393.76		393.76		
Bank Account	2,157.17		2,157.17		
VAT Liability	90.68		90.68		
		2,753.81			2,753.81
Current Liabilities					
Creditors : Short Term	566.12		566.12		
		566.12			566.12
Current Assets less Current Liabilities:		2,187.69			2,187.69
Total Assets less Current Liabilities:		2,187.69			2,187.69
Long Term Liabilities					
		0.00			0.00
Total Assets less Total Liabilities:		2,187.69			2,187.69
Capital & Reserves					
Share Capital	3,000.00		3,000.00		
P&L Account	(812.31)		(812.31)		
		2,187.69			2,187.69

3.6   The Audit Trail

The Audit Trail report is run as follows:

Company – Financials (in the links section) – Audit (on the menu at the top of the screen)

The Audit Trail shows a list of every debit and credit that has been posted onto the system. Even if data is deleted using the maintenance tool, it will still show up on the audit trail. This makes it easier to trace transactions and ensure that things have been posted correctly.

This is a very important report and one that you should practice creating.

No	Type	A/C	N/C	Dept	Details	Date	Ref	Net	Tax	T/C	Pd	Paid	V	B	Bank Rec. Date
						Date: 16/01/2018		**TotalPhoto Ltd.**							**Page:** 1
						Time: 19:28:48		**Audit Trail (Detailed)**							
Date From:		01/01/1980										**Customer From:**			
Date To:		31/12/2019										**Customer To:**	ZZZZZZZZ		
Transaction From:		1										**Supplier From:**			
Transaction To:		99,999,999										**Supplier To:**	ZZZZZZZZ		
Exclude Deleted Tran:		No													
1	JD	1200				30/09/2017	O/Bal	668.80	0.00		Y	668.80	-		30/09/2017
		1	1200	0	Opening Balance			668.80	0.00	T9		668.80	-		
2	JC	9998				30/09/2017	O/Bal	668.80	0.00		Y	668.80	-		
		2	9998	0	Opening Balance			668.80	0.00	T9		668.80	-		
3	JD	1230				30/09/2017	O/Bal	252.00	0.00		Y	252.00	-		30/09/2017
		3	1230	0	Opening Balance			252.00	0.00	T9		252.00	-		
4	JC	9998				30/09/2017	O/Bal	252.00	0.00		Y	252.00	-		
		4	9998	0	Opening Balance			252.00	0.00	T9		252.00	-		
5	JC	2200				30/09/2017	O/Bal	369.36	0.00		Y	369.36	-		
		5	2200	0	Opening Balance			369.36	0.00	T9		369.36	-		
6	JD	9998				30/09/2017	O/Bal	369.36	0.00		Y	369.36	-		
		6	9998	0	Opening Balance			369.36	0.00	T9		369.36	-		
7	JD	2201				30/09/2017	O/Bal	382.56	0.00		Y	382.56	-		
		7	2201	0	Opening Balance			382.56	0.00	T9		382.56	-		
8	JC	9998				30/09/2017	O/Bal	382.56	0.00		Y	382.56	-		
		8	9998	0	Opening Balance			382.56	0.00	T9		382.56	-		
9	JC	3000				30/09/2017	O/Bal	1,000.00	0.00		Y	1,000.00	-		
		9	3000	0	Opening Balance			1,000.00	0.00	T9		1,000.00	-		
10	JD	9998				30/09/2017	O/Bal	1,000.00	0.00		Y	1,000.00	-		
		10	9998	0	Opening Balance			1,000.00	0.00	T9		1,000.00	-		
11	JD	5000				30/09/2017	O/Bal	1,568.90	0.00		Y	1,568.90	-		
		11	5000	0	Opening Balance			1,568.90	0.00	T9		1,568.90	-		

4 Bank and cash reports

4.1 Bank and Cash Reports

When producing Bank and Cash reports, it is important that you make sure you have the correct account highlighted in the **Bank Module.**

If the **Bank Current Account** is highlighted, then the reports that you produce will present information on the Bank Current Account.

If the **Cash Account** is highlighted, the reports you produce will present information on the Cash Account.

In the AAT assessment, you may be required to produce reports for both the Bank Current account and the Cash account. Please ensure that you select the correct one as incorrect information being uploaded to the exam platform will result in a loss of marks.

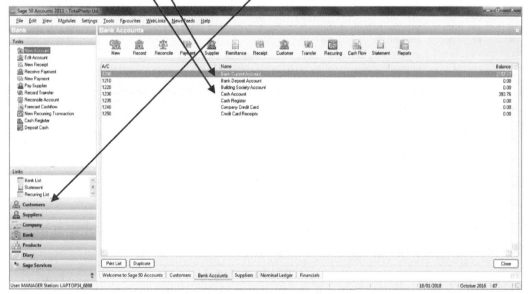

4.2 Bank Payments Analysis

The Bank Payments Analysis report can be accessed as follows:

Bank (make sure the current account is highlighted) – Reports – Bank Payments Reports – Bank Payments

This report will show an analysis of all payments that have gone through the Bank Current Account.

Date:	16/01/2018				**TotalPhoto Ltd.**							Page:	1
Time:	19:39:54				**Day Books: Bank Payments (Detailed)**								

Date From:	01/01/1980									Bank From:	1200
Date To:	31/12/2019									Bank To:	1200

Transaction From:	1							N/C From:	
Transaction To:	99,999,999							N/C To:	99999999

Dept From:	0
Dept To:	999

Bank: 1200   Currency: Pound Sterling

No	Type	N/C	Date	Ref	Details	Dept	Net £	Tax £ T/C	Gross £ V B	Bank Rec. Date
48	BP	5001	30/09/2017		Specialist Photo	0	34.00	6.80 T1	40.80 N N	
49	BP	5003	30/09/2017		Stationery	0	56.50	11.30 T1	67.80 N N	
52	BP	7004	30/09/2017		Wages	0	345.60	0.00 T9	345.60 · N	
53	BP	7502	30/09/2017		Telephone	0	37.88	7.57 T1	45.45 N N	
54	BP	6201	30/09/2017		Advertising	0	83.33	16.67 T1	100.00 N N	
55	BP	7201	30/09/2017		Gas	0	45.33	9.07 T1	54.40 N N	
56	BP	7200	30/09/2017		Electricity	0	26.67	5.33 T1	32.00 N N	
						Totals £	629.31	56.74	686.05	

4.3 Bank Receipts Analysis

The Bank Receipts Analysis is similar but shows receipts rather than payments and can be viewed by following:

Bank (make sure the current account is highlighted) – Reports – Bank Receipts Reports – Bank Receipts

This report will show an analysis of all receipts that have come into the Bank Current Account.

Date:	16/01/2018				**TotalPhoto Ltd.**							Page:	1
Time:	19:41:40				**Day Books: Bank Receipts (Detailed)**								

Date From:	01/01/1980									Bank From:	1200
Date To:	31/12/2019									Bank To:	1200

Transaction From:	1							N/C From:	
Transaction To:	99,999,999							N/C To:	99999999

Dept From:	0
Dept To:	999

Bank: 1200   Currency: Pound Sterling

No	Type	N/C	Date	Ref	Details	Dept	Net £	Tax £ T/C	Gross £ V B	Bank Rec. Date
46	BR	4000	30/09/2017		Colour Print	0	12.00	2.40 T1	14.40 N N	
47	BR	4003	30/09/2017		School Photos (Set 2)	0	28.00	5.60 T1	33.60 N N	
50	BR	4003	30/09/2017		School Photo	0	12.50	2.50 T1	15.00 N N	
51	BR	4002	30/09/2017		Corporate	0	187.50	37.50 T1	225.00 N N	
						Totals £	240.00	48.00	288.00	

4.4 Bank Payments and Receipts Analysis

The Bank Payments and Receipts Analysis report shows both payments and receipts:

Bank (make sure the current account is highlighted) – Reports – Bank Payments and Receipts Reports – Bank Payments and Receipts

This report will show an analysis of all receipts and payments that have passed through the Bank Current Account.

Date: 16/01/2018				**TotalPhoto Ltd.**				Page: 1	
Time: 19:43:14				**Bank Payments & Receipts by Bank Account**					

Date From: 01/01/1980

Date To: 31/12/2019

Transaction No From: 1

Transaction No To: 99,999,999

** NOTE: All values shown on this report are in the Bank Account's operating Currency **

Bank Code: 1200   Bank Name: Bank Current Account

No	Type	Date	N/C	Ref	Details	Net Amount	Tax Amount	Gross Amount	B	Bank Rec. Date
46	BR	30/09/2017	4000		Colour Print	12.00	2.40	14.40	N	
47	BR	30/09/2017	4003		School Photos (Set 2)	28.00	5.60	33.60	N	
48	BP	30/09/2017	5001		Specialist Photo Paper	-34.00	-6.80	-40.80	N	
49	BP	30/09/2017	5003		Stationery	-56.50	-11.30	-67.80	N	
50	BR	30/09/2017	4003		School Photo	12.50	2.50	15.00	N	
51	BR	30/09/2017	4002		Corporate	187.50	37.50	225.00	N	
52	BP	30/09/2017	7004		Wages	-345.60	0.00	-345.60	N	
53	BP	30/09/2017	7502		Telephone	-37.88	-7.57	-45.45	N	
54	BP	30/09/2017	6201		Advertising	-83.33	-16.67	-100.00	N	
55	BP	30/09/2017	7201		Gas	-45.33	-9.07	-54.40	N	
56	BP	30/09/2017	7200		Electricity	-26.67	-5.33	-32.00	N	
						-389.31	-8.74	-398.05		
						-389.31	-8.74	-398.05		

4.5 Cash Analysis reports

To create cash analysis reports, you simply follow the same process but you select the Cash Account from the bank module.

The Cash Payments Analysis report is accessed using:

Bank (make sure the cash account is highlighted) – Reports – Cash Payments Reports – Cash Payments

This report will show an analysis of all cash payments that have been entered in the Cash Account.

Date: 16/01/2018				**TotalPhoto Ltd.**					Page: 1	
Time: 19:46:58				**Day Books: Cash Payments (Detailed)**						

Date From: 01/01/1980   DateTo: 31/12/2019

Bank From: 1230   Bank To: 1230

Transaction From: 1   Transaction To: 99,999,999

N/C From: N/C To: 99999999

Dept From: 0   Dept To: 999

Bank: 1230   Currency: Pound Sterling

No	Type	N/C	Date	Ref	Details	Dept	Net £	Tax £	T/C	Gross £	V	B	Bank Rec. Date
57	CP	7801	30/09/2017	11762	Window Cleaner	0	4.00	0.00	T0	4.00	N	-	
58	CP	8205	30/09/2017	11763	Tea and milk	0	2.65	0.00	T0	2.65	N	-	
59	CP	8201	30/09/2017	11764	Magazine	0	3.00	0.00	T0	3.00	N	-	
60	CP	7501	30/09/2017	11765	Stamps	0	3.60	0.00	T0	3.60	N	-	
61	CP	7504	30/09/2017	11766	Pens	0	1.66	0.33	T1	1.99	N	-	
62	CP	7400	30/09/2017	11767	Taxi Fare	0	6.67	1.33	T1	8.00	N	-	
						Totals £	21.58	1.66		23.24			

The **Cash Receipts Analysis** report is run using the following:

Bank (make sure the current account is highlighted) – Reports – Cash Receipts Reports – Cash Receipts

This report will show an analysis of all cash receipts that have been entered in the Cash Account.

Date:	16/01/2018				**TotalPhoto Ltd.**								Page:	1	
Time:	19:49:05				**Day Books: Cash Receipts (Detailed)**										

Date From:	01/01/1980										Bank From:	1230	
Date To:	31/12/2019										Bank To:	1230	

Transaction From:	1								N/C From:	
Transaction To:	99,999,999								N/C To:	99999999

Dept From:	0
Dept To:	999

Bank:	1230		Currency:	Pound Sterling										Bank Rec.
No	Type	N/C	Date	Ref	Details	Dept	Net £	Tax	£ T/C	Gross	£ V	B	Date
63	CR	4000	30/09/2017		Family photo	0	20.00		4.00 T1	24.00	N	-	
64	CR	4000	30/09/2017		Individual photo	0	11.67		2.33 T1	14.00	N	-	
65	CR	4003	30/09/2017		Nursery photos	0	17.50		3.50 T1	21.00	N	-	
66	CR	4002	30/09/2017		Corporate photos	0	70.83		14.17 T1	85.00	N	-	
67	CR	4003	30/09/2017		School Photos	0	17.50		3.50 T1	21.00	N	-	
						Totals £	137.50	27.50		165.00			

This is just a small selection of the reports that are available to view within Sage.

Keep practising generating reports and exporting these to PDF format, you will need them in your assessment!

📖 Case study

Chrissie has now used the data she has entered into the computerised accounting software to produce a number of reports, which show the customers and suppliers of TotalPhoto Ltd, recent transactions and the company's financial situation.

Some of these reports will enable Matt and Stuart to make decisions about the business and others will prove useful for required accounting procedures.

Chrissie is also confident that the information provided is accurate due to the nature of computerised accounting and, moving forward, she will look to use the data more widely by exporting it into other formats.

Matt and Stuart are very happy with the software's impact on TotalPhoto Ltd and with Chrissie's understanding of Sage.

Mock Assessment 1 – Access Award in Accounting Software

Introduction

The following is a Mock Assessment to be attempted in exam conditions.

You should attempt and aim to complete EVERY task.

Read every task carefully to make sure you understand what is required.

The assessment includes 6 tasks across two sections:

Section 1 – Task 1 consists of a series of short answer questions.

Section 2 – Tasks 2 – 6 will ask you to process transactions using computerised accounting software, you will then be required to produce reports.

Any documents produced in respect of this assessment should be in one of the following formats: XLS, XLSX, CSV, PDF. In the live assessment, any documents that are submitted in alternative file formats will not be marked.

In the live assessment, you will be required to upload all of the requested reports from section 2. If you fail to upload your evidence, it cannot be marked so it is important to familiarise yourself with the exam software to ensure that this is done correctly.

ALL documents should be saved and titled with the following information:

- Evidence number
- Your name
- Your AAT membership number

For example, evidence 1 should be saved with the file name:

Evidence 1 - Joe Bloggs - 12345678

The time allowed for this assessment is **2 hours.** You should allow a minimum of 15 minutes at the end of the assessment to upload your evidence.

1 Mock Assessment Questions

Section 1: Task 1 (20 marks)

Task 1a (5 marks)

Match the features in the picklist below to the relevant heading within the table.

Off the shelf software	Bespoke software

Picklist:

Updates are made regularly and with ease

Costs are fixed and can be easily budgeted for

Reporting is tailored specifically for the needs of your business

Set up and implementation is minimal

The system is tailored specifically for the processes of the business

Task 1b (2 marks)

Identify which TWO of the following are advantages of cloud based accounting software.

Cloud based accounting software…..	✓
…..produces financial reports in real-time	
…..requires memory on the server to store financial information	
…..can produce reports that are specifically tailored to your business	
…..can be backed up at any time to your computer	
…..allows users to access financial information wherever they are	

Task 1c (3 marks)

Which **three** of the following would be indicators of a manual bookkeeping system?

Indicators:	✓
It can be done anywhere	
It is a cheap way of accounting for a small business	
It is quicker	
It is more accurate	
Reports can be produced easily	
You don't need to worry about the software crashing	

Task 1d (3 marks)

Place the correct threats to data security from the picklist below next to each of the following definitions.

Definition	Threat
Unauthorised access or control to a computer network with a motive of altering information or stealing information for personal gain.	
Being contacted by someone via email who is posing as HMRC and asking for you to provide your bank details to receive a refund.	
A computer program which attaches itself to files and then duplicates itself to cause harm to your computer.	

Picklist:

A Virus

Hacking

Phishing

Task 1e (2 marks)

Which **two** of the following can protect accounting software against threats?

	✓
Only have one log in so that you know exactly who has access to the system	
Have unlimited access for all registered users of the accounting system	
Encrypt files so that they are only readable by authorised users	
Ensure that passwords are changed regularly	

Task 1f (2 marks)

Which **two** of the following reports would not show your sales figure?

Report	✓
Trial Balance	
Aged creditors report	
Profit and loss report	
Balance sheet report	

Task 1g (3 marks)

Which **three** of the following reports would show a sale made in cash?

Report	✓
Cash payments analysis	
Aged creditors report	
Cash receipts analysis	
Balance sheet report	
Audit trail	
Sales analysis	

Section 2:

Information

How Two Ltd. is a small owner managed computer consumables company based in London. The owner, John Bennett, has decided to use an accounting software package from 1st January 20XX onwards.

Information relating to the business:

Business name:	How Two Ltd.
Business address:	1 Baker Street London WC1 8QT
Business owner:	John Bennett
Accounting period end:	31st December (each year)
VAT registration number:	485 4212 68
VAT rate:	Standard rate of VAT at 20%

You have been asked to carry out the bookkeeping tasks for January 20XX only.

All documents have been checked for accuracy and have been authorised by John Bennett.

Before you start the assessment, you should:

- Set up the business name, address, owner and accounting period

- If required by your software, please add your VAT number and rate

- Set the system software date as **31st January of the current year.**

- Set the financial year to start on **1st January of the current year.**

Depending on the requirements of your software, you may be unable to set the opening balance to the date shown. If this is the case, you may select an alternative opening balance date. Your result will not be affected.

Please ensure that the reports prepared in task 6 cover an appropriate period in relation to the dates you have set.

The setup of the software does not form part of the assessment standards, so your training provider may assist you with this. Marks will not be awarded for the setup procedure as your software may not allow you to carry out all of the setup procedures requested.

Task 2 (20 marks)

Task 2a (16 marks)

Refer to the list of general ledger accounts below, taken from the spreadsheet that How Two Ltd. have been using.

Set up general ledger records for each account, entering opening balances (if applicable) as at 1st January 20XX.

Make sure you select, amend or create appropriate general ledger account codes.

Opening trial balance as at 1st January 20XX

Account names	Debit £	Credit £
Office Equipment – cost	7840.00	
Motor Vehicles – cost	12,370.00	
Bank current account	3,745.00	
Cash account	750.00	
Loan		12,500.00
Capital		15,000.00
Drawings	NIL	
Sales Tax Control Account		NIL
Purchase Tax Control Account	NIL	
Sales – Computers		NIL
Sales – Computer Accessories		NIL
Purchases – Computers	NIL	
Purchases – Computer Accessories	NIL	
Telephone	345.00	
Premises Insurance	NIL	
Computer Insurance	NIL	
Wages	2,450.00	
Bank Charges	NIL	
	27,500.00	**27,500.00**

Task 2b (4 marks)

How Two Ltd. have been using the following list of general ledger accounts.

Set up general ledger records for each account, ensuring that you amend or create appropriate general ledger account codes. The accounting software that you are using may not have these accounts as standard.

Account Names
Sales – Printers
Purchases – Printers
Wages – Sales Commission
Admin Expenses

Task 3 (10 marks)

Refer to the following bank statement. Use the accounting software to enter the transactions.

QC Bank

QC Street, London

To: How Two Ltd.

  1 Baker Street
London   Sort Code 77-88-99
WC1 8QT   Account No 92836152   **Date:** 31 January 20XX

Statement of Account

Date	Details	Notes	Payments	Receipts	Balance
20XX			£	£	£
1 Jan	Bal b/f				3745.00
3 Jan	IT Geeks DD - Computers			1800.00	5545.00
4 Jan	Deposit - Redshaw Cables (Accessories)			425.00	5970.00
6 Jan	DD – Wages	*	980.00		4990.00
9 Jan	PC's R Us - Computers		550.00		4440.00
10 Jan	BACS – Telephone		87.90		4352.10
11 Jan	Faster Payment – Bank Loan	*	1500.00		2852.10
21 Jan	DD – Computer Accessories		75.00		2777.10
22 Jan	DD – Computer Insurance		150.00		2627.10
24 Jan	Bank charges	*	15.00		2612.10
28 Jan	DD – Premises Insurance	*	55.00		2557.10

Please note: All items except for those marked with a * in the notes column, include VAT at the standard rate of 20%.

Items marked with a * do not include VAT.

Task 4 (10 marks)

Refer to the following five cash payments and enter them into the accounting software.

Redshaw Cables (VAT No. 4585 2279 00)
17 High Street
Manchester M1 6RS
Tel: 0161 741 2962
Fax: 0161 741 2963
Date: 15th January 20XX
Invoice Number: Inv2451
To: How Two Ltd.

	£
Computer Accessories	125.00
VAT	25.00
Total	150.00

IT Geeks Ltd. (VAT No. 3275 4567 88)
11 Mountjoy St
London W12 6RS
Tel: 020 4580 6699
Date: 19th January 20XX
Invoice Number: F47/INV
To: How Two Ltd.

	£
Printer	199.00
VAT	39.80
Total	238.80

Cable Comms (VAT No. 4585 2279 00)
176 Statton Road
Manchester M1 7UV
Tel: 0161 851 4872
Fax: 0161 851 8900
Date: 24th January 20XX
Invoice Number: TEL9901X
To: How Two Ltd.

	£
Telephone Bill	45.45
VAT	9.09
Total	54.54

AdminaMinute (VAT No. 3275 4567 88)
11 High Street
London L1 4SE
Tel: 020 8877 6655
Date: 27th January 20XX
Invoice Number: 4521X
To: How Two Ltd.

	£
Admin Expenses	34.80
VAT	6.96
Total	41.76

IT Crowd (VAT No. 2126 5487 01)
19 Bond Street
Chichester CH1 6MT
Tel: 0141 228 5876
Date: 28th January 20XX
Invoice Number: 2344
To: How Two Ltd.

	£
Printer	85.00
VAT	17.00
Total	102.00

Task 5 (10 marks)

Refer to the following e-mail from John Bennett and enter the five transactions into the accounting software.

From: John Bennett

To: Accounting Technician

Date: 31st January 20XX

Subject: January Transactions

Hi

The following transactions were received into the cash account this month:

Date	Description	Net	VAT	Gross
2nd Jan	Computer	180.00	36.00	216.00
8th Jan	Printer	99.00	19.80	118.80
10th Jan	Printer	75.00	15.00	90.00
19th Jan	Accessories	24.50	4.90	29.40
25th Jan	Computer	165.00	33.00	198.00

Please could you process them into the accounting software.

Kind Regards,

John

Task 6 (10 marks)

Generate the following documents using the accounting software. Save/upload them as required.

Document and Reports	Save/Upload as:
Computer accessories purchases general ledger for the month of January 20XX	Evidence 1 – Name – AAT Number
Printer sales general ledger for the month of January 20XX	Evidence 2 – Name – AAT Number
Trial Balance as at 31st January 20XX	Evidence 3 – Name – AAT Number
Bank Payments Analysis for the month of January 20XX	Evidence 4 – Name – AAT Number
A detailed audit trail showing all transactions for the month of January 20XX	Evidence 5 – Name – AAT Number

Mock Assessment 2 – Access Award in Accounting Software

Introduction

The following is a Mock Assessment to be attempted in exam conditions.

You should attempt and aim to complete EVERY task.

Read every task carefully to make sure you understand what is required.

The assessment includes 6 tasks across two sections:

Section 1 – Task 1 consists of a series of short answer questions.

Section 2 – Tasks 2 – 6 will ask you to process transactions using computerised accounting software, you will then be required to produce reports.

Any documents produced in respect of this assessment should be in one of the following formats: XLS, XLSX, CSV, PDF. In the live assessment, any documents that are submitted in alternative file formats will not be marked.

In the live assessment, you will be required to upload all of the requested reports from section 2. If you fail to upload your evidence, it cannot be marked so it is important to familiarise yourself with the exam software to ensure that this is done correctly.

ALL documents should be saved and titled with the following information:

- Evidence number
- Your name
- Your AAT membership number

For example, evidence 1 should be saved with the file name:

Evidence 1 - Joe Bloggs - 12345678

The time allowed for this assessment is **2 hours.** You should allow a minimum of 15 minutes at the end of the assessment to upload your evidence.

1 Mock Assessment Questions

Section 1: Task 1 (20 marks)

Task 1a (5 marks)

Match the features in the picklist below to the relevant heading within the table.

Traditional Accounting Software	Cloud Software

Picklist:

No need for an internet connection

Can be paid in monthly instalments with no upfront fees for hardware

Users of the system can work from anywhere with an internet connection

All financial information is securely stored on the server

Can be synced with your phone or tablet so that you can work on the move

Task 1b (2 marks)

Identify which **two** of the following are advantages of bespoke software in comparison to 'of the shelf' software.

Bespoke accounting software…..	✓
…..can evolve over time to match your changing requirements	
…..is available immediately and therefore is more efficient	
…..requires less in house training	
…..is cheaper in comparison to 'off the shelf' software	
…..has no extra per user fees as your business grows	

Task 1c (3 marks)

Which **three** of the following would be indicators of cloud based software?

Indicators	✓
Development and installation will only take about two weeks	
Updates are run automatically and are included in the price	
Accounting can be done anywhere so long as there is an internet connection	
Developed and built to meet your specific needs; it is flexible	
Can be easily modified to match your specific requirements	
Financial information produced is always up to date and current	

Task 1d (3 marks)

Place the correct threats to data security from the picklist below next to each of the following statements.

Definition	Threat
One of the clerks has been processing transactions all day and then they delete them by accident	
You have been working on a project for nearly a month. When you come to work on it again and try to open it, an error message comes up to say that there's something wrong with the file	
You have been processing month end adjustments all morning and then your screen freezes and the software shuts down automatically	

Picklist

Corrupt file

Software crashes

Accidental deletion

Task 1e (2 marks)

Which **two** of the following can protect accounting software against threats?

	✓
Give all users of the system a specific way of setting their password so that you can access it on their behalf even if they leave suddenly	
Implement firewalls on all hardware and software	
Enlist different levels of access rights depending on the user	
Ensure that a backup is taken once a week in case of a fire or flood	

Task 1f (2 marks)

Which **two** of the following reports would show your sales figure?

Report	✓
Trial Balance	
Aged creditors report	
Profit and loss report	
Balance sheet report	

Task 1g (3 marks)

Which **three** of the following reports would not show a sale made in cash?

Report	✓
Cash payments analysis	
Aged creditors report	
Cash receipts analysis	
Balance sheet report	
Audit trail	
Sales analysis	

Section 2:

Information

Cakes Away is a small owner managed bakery based in Manchester. The owner, Carol Jones, has decided to use an accounting software package from 1st July 20XX onwards.

Information relating to the business:

Business name:	Cakes Away
Business address:	163 Shearwater Road Manchester M2 5SR
Business owner:	Carol Jones
Accounting period end:	30th June (each year)
VAT registration number:	228 6484 21
VAT rate:	Standard rate of VAT at 20%

You have been asked to carry out the bookkeeping tasks for July 20XX only.

All documents have been checked for accuracy and have been authorised by Carol Jones.

Before you start the assessment, you should:

- Set up the business name, address, owner and accounting period

- If required by your software, please add your VAT number and rate

- Set the system software date as **31st July of the current year.**

- Set the financial year to start on **1st July of the current year.**

Depending on the requirements of your software, you may be unable to set the opening balance to the date shown. If this is the case, you may select an alternative opening balance date. Your result will not be affected.

Please ensure that the reports prepared in task 6 cover an appropriate period in relation to the dates you have set.

The setup of the software does not form part of the assessment standards, so your training provider may assist you with this. Marks will not be awarded for the setup procedure as your software may not allow you to carry out all of the setup procedures requested.

Task 2 (20 marks)

Task 2a (16 marks)

Refer to the list of general ledger accounts below, taken from the spreadsheet that Cakes Away have been using.

Set up general ledger records for each account, entering opening balances (if applicable) as at 1st July 20XX.

Make sure you select, amend or create appropriate general ledger account codes.

Opening trial balance as at 1st July 20XX

Account names	Debit £	Credit £
Equipment – cost	9,450.75	
Equipment – accumulated depreciation		1,375.60
Motor Vehicles – cost	15,788.90	
Motor Vehicles – accumulated depreciation		4,752.30
Bank current account	2,425.80	
Cash account	625.45	
Loan		14,000.00
Capital		8,163.00
Drawings	NIL	
Sales Tax Control Account		NIL
Purchase Tax Control Account	NIL	
Sales – Wedding Cakes		NIL
Sales – Birthday Cakes		NIL
Purchases – Ingredients	NIL	
Purchases – Accessories	NIL	
Heat and light	NIL	
Premises Insurance	NIL	
Bank Charges	NIL	
	28,290.90	28,290.90

Task 2b (4 marks)

Cakes Away have been using the following list of general ledger accounts.

Set up general ledger records for each account, ensuring that you amend or create appropriate general ledger account codes. The accounting software that you are using may not have these accounts as standard.

Account Names
Sales – Cupcakes
Bank Interest Received
Events costs
Admin Expenses

Task 3 (10 marks)

Refer to the following bank statement.

Use the accounting software to enter the transactions.

<table>
<tr><td colspan="6" align="center">**QC Bank**</td></tr>
<tr><td colspan="6" align="center">**QC Street, London**</td></tr>
<tr><td colspan="6">To: Cakes Away
   163 Shearwater Road
   Manchester   Sort Code 33-44-55
   M2 5SR   Account No 98765432   **Date:** 31 July 20XX</td></tr>
<tr><td colspan="6" align="center">**Statement of Account**</td></tr>
<tr><td>**Date**</td><td>**Details**</td><td>**Notes**</td><td>**Payments**</td><td>**Receipts**</td><td>**Balance**</td></tr>
<tr><td>**20XX**</td><td></td><td></td><td>£</td><td>£</td><td>£</td></tr>
<tr><td>1 Jul</td><td>Bal b/f</td><td></td><td></td><td></td><td>2,425.80</td></tr>
<tr><td>3 Jul</td><td>Deposit - A Parker (Birthday)</td><td></td><td></td><td>75.00</td><td>2,500.80</td></tr>
<tr><td>4 Jul</td><td>FP – H Eastwood (Wedding)</td><td></td><td></td><td>325.00</td><td>2,825.80</td></tr>
<tr><td>6 Jul</td><td>Drawings</td><td>*</td><td>131.00</td><td></td><td>2,694.80</td></tr>
<tr><td>9 Jul</td><td>The Flour Mill (Ingredients)</td><td></td><td>76.26</td><td></td><td>2,618.54</td></tr>
<tr><td>10 Jul</td><td>Bank Interest Received</td><td>*</td><td></td><td>9.74</td><td>2,628.28</td></tr>
<tr><td>11 Jul</td><td>Faster Payment – Bank Loan</td><td>*</td><td>500.00</td><td></td><td>2,128.28</td></tr>
<tr><td>21 Jul</td><td>Pretty Cakes (Accessories)</td><td></td><td>34.98</td><td></td><td>2,093.30</td></tr>
<tr><td>22 Jul</td><td>Bake that Cake (Ingredients)</td><td></td><td>67.85</td><td></td><td>2,025.45</td></tr>
<tr><td>24 Jul</td><td>Bank charges</td><td>*</td><td>7.56</td><td></td><td>2,017.89</td></tr>
<tr><td>28 Jul</td><td>DD – Premises Insurance</td><td>*</td><td>35.00</td><td></td><td>1,982.89</td></tr>
</table>

Please note: All items except for those marked with a * in the notes column, include VAT at the standard rate of 20%.

Items marked with a * do not include VAT.

Task 4 (10 marks)

Refer to the following five cash payments and enter them into the accounting software.

Events City Walk (VAT No. 4257 7940 00)		**HobbyCroft (VAT No. 4875 2234 88)**	
42 Talbot Way		201 The Grove	
Manchester M1 6SU		London WC6 9ST	
Tel: 0161 872 2211		Tel: 020 8765 4321	
Date: 15th July 20XX		Date: 19th July 20XX	
Invoice Number: Inv1225		Invoice Number: INV00156	
To: Cakes Away		**To: Cakes Away**	
	£		£
Event Pitch (Full day)	50.00	**Cake Accessories**	48.00
VAT	10.00	**VAT**	9.60
Total	60.00	**Total**	57.60

Toppers R Us (VAT No. 3321 4457 00)		**Food Hall Ltd. (VAT No. 2750 6677 88)**	
82 Hazel Street		Unit 4 High Hill Industrial Estate	
Manchester M27 4LE		London L1 8FY	
Tel: 0161 776 9321		Tel: 020 9182 7364	
Fax: 0161 776 9231			
Date: 24th July 20XX		Date: 27th July 20XX	
Invoice Number: TOP2211		Invoice Number: IN0765V	
To: Cakes Away		**To: Cakes Away**	
	£		£
Cake Toppers	31.05	**Admin Expenses**	76.82
VAT	6.21	**VAT**	15.36
Total	37.26	**Total**	92.18

Energy World (VAT No. 4532 0212 01)	
61 Merseyway	
Newcastle NL1 5TZ	
Tel: 0171 678 9010	
Date: 28th July 20XX	
Invoice Number: 1890	
To: Cakes Away	
	£
Heat and Light	125.40
VAT	25.08
Total	150.48

Task 5 (10 marks)

Refer to the following e-mail from Carol Jones and enter the five transactions into the accounting software.

From: Carol Jones

To: Accounting Technician

Date: 31st July 20XX

Subject: July Transactions

Hi

The following transactions were received into the cash account this month:

Date	Description	Net	VAT	Gross
2nd Jul	Birthday Cake	65.00	13.00	78.00
8th Jul	Wedding Cake	395.00	79.00	474.00
10th Jul	Cupcakes	35.00	7.00	42.00
19th Jul	Wedding Cake	485.00	97.00	582.00
25th Jul	Cupcakes	70.00	14.00	84.00

Please could you process them into the accounting software.

Many thanks,

Carol

Task 6 (10 marks)

Generate the following documents using the accounting software. Save/upload them as required.

Document and Reports	Save/Upload as:
Wedding Cakes sales general ledger for the month of July 20XX	Evidence 1 – Name – AAT Number
Cake Accessories purchases general ledger for the month of July 20XX	Evidence 2 – Name – AAT Number
Trial Balance as at 31st July 20XX	Evidence 3 – Name – AAT Number
Cash Payments Analysis for the month of July 20XX	Evidence 4 – Name – AAT Number
A detailed audit trail showing all transactions for the month of July 20XX	Evidence 5 – Name – AAT Number

Mock Assessments – Access Award in Accounting Software: Answers

1 Mock Assessment 1 Answers

Section 1: Task 1 (20 marks)

Task 1a (5 marks)

Off the shelf software	Bespoke software
Updates are made regularly and with ease	Reporting is tailored specifically for the needs of your business
Costs are fixed and can be easily budgeted for	The system is tailored specifically for the processes of the business
Set up and implementation is minimal	

Task 1b (2 marks)

Cloud based accounting software…..	✓
…..produces financial reports in real-time	✓
…..requires memory on the server to store financial information	
…..can produce reports that are specifically tailored to your business	
…..can be backed up at any time to your computer	
…..allows users to access financial information wherever they are	✓

Task 1c (3 marks)

Indicators:	✓
It can be done anywhere	✓
It is a cheap way of accounting for a small business	✓
It is quicker	
It is more accurate	
Reports can be produced easily	
You don't need to worry about the software crashing	✓

Task 1d (3 marks)

Definition	Threat
Unauthorised access or control to a computer network with a motive of altering information or stealing information for personal gain.	Hacking
Being contacted by someone via email who is posing as HMRC and asking for you to provide your bank details to receive a refund.	Phishing
A computer program which attaches itself to files and then duplicates itself to cause harm to your computer.	A Virus

Task 1e (2 marks)

	✓
Only have one log in so that you know exactly who has access to the system	
Have unlimited access for all registered users of the accounting system	
Encrypt files so that they are only readable by authorised users	✓
Ensure that passwords are changed regularly	✓

Task 1f (2 marks)

Report	✓
Trial Balance	
Aged creditors report	✓
Profit and loss report	
Balance sheet report	✓

Task 1g (3 marks)

Report	✓
Cash payments analysis	
Aged creditors report	
Cash receipts analysis	✓
Balance sheet report	
Audit trail	✓
Sales analysis	✓

Section 2:

Tasks 2–6 (60 marks)

Evidence 1 – Computer Accessories Purchases analysis

Date:	18/01/2018			How Two Ltd.				Page:	1
Time:	20:46:51			**Nominal Activity**					

Date From:	01/01/2018	N/C From:	5001
Date To:	31/01/2018	N/C To:	5001

Transaction From:	1
Transaction To:	99,999,999

N/C:	5001		Name:	Purchases - Computer Accessories			Account Balance:			187.50 DR

No	Type	Date	Account	Ref	Details	Dept	T/C	Value	Debit	Credit	V	B
23	BP	21/01/2018	1200	DD	Computer Accessories	0	T1	62.50	62.50		N	N
27	CP	15/01/2018	1230		Computer Accessories	0	T1	125.00	125.00		N	-
							Totals:		187.50			
							History Balance:		187.50			

Evidence 2 – Printer Sales analysis

Date:	18/01/2018			How Two Ltd.				Page:	1
Time:	20:49:19			**Nominal Activity**					

Date From:	01/01/2018	N/C From:	4002
Date To:	31/01/2018	N/C To:	4002

Transaction From:	1
Transaction To:	99,999,999

N/C:	4002		Name:	Sales - Printers			Account Balance:			174.00 CR

No	Type	Date	Account	Ref	Details	Dept	T/C	Value	Debit	Credit	V	B
33	CR	08/01/2018	1230		Printer	0	T1	99.00		99.00	N	-
34	CR	10/01/2018	1230		Printer	0	T1	75.00		75.00	N	-
							Totals:			174.00		
							History Balance:			174.00		

Evidence 3 – Trial Balance

Date:	18/01/2018	How Two Ltd.		Page:	1
Time:	20:51:05	Period Trial Balance			

To Period: Month 12, December 2018

N/C	Name	Debit	Credit
0030	Office Equipment - cost	7,840.00	
0050	Motor Vehicles - cost	12,370.00	
1200	Bank Current Account	2,557.10	
1230	Cash Account	815.10	
2200	Sales Tax Control Account		479.53
2201	Purchase Tax Control Account	241.67	
2300	Loan		11,000.00
3000	Capital		15,000.00
4000	Sales - Computers		1,845.00
4001	Sales - Computer Accessories		378.67
4002	Sales - Printers		174.00
5000	Purchases - Computers	458.33	
5001	Purchases - Computer Accessories	187.50	
5002	Purchases - Printers	284.00	
7004	Wages	3,430.00	
7104	Premises Insurance	55.00	
7105	Computer Insurance	125.00	
7502	Telephone	463.70	
7506	Admin Expenses	34.80	
7901	Bank Charges	15.00	
	Totals:	28,877.20	28,877.20

Evidence 4 – Bank payments analysis

Date:	18/01/2018	How Two Ltd.		Page:	1
Time:	20:53:09	Day Books: Bank Payments (Detailed)			

Date From:	01/01/2018		Bank From:	1200
DateTo:	31/01/2018		Bank To:	1200

Transaction From:	1		N/C From:	
Transaction To:	99,999,999		N/C To:	99999999

Dept From:	0
Dept To:	999

Bank: 1200   **Currency:** Pound Sterling

No	Type	N/C	Date	Ref	Details	Dept	Net £	Tax £ T/C	Gross £ V B	Bank Rec. Date
19	BP	7004	06/01/2018	DD	Wages	0	980.00	0.00 T0	980.00 N N	
20	BP	5000	09/01/2018		PCs R Us	0	458.33	91.67 T1	550.00 N N	
21	BP	7502	10/01/2018	BACS	Telephone	0	73.25	14.65 T1	87.90 N N	
22	BP	2300	11/01/2018	FP	Bank Loan	0	1,500.00	0.00 T0	1,500.00 N N	
23	BP	5001	21/01/2018	DD	Computer	0	62.50	12.50 T1	75.00 N N	
24	BP	7105	22/01/2018	DD	Computer Insurance	0	125.00	25.00 T1	150.00 N N	
25	BP	7901	24/01/2018	Chgs	Bank Charges	0	15.00	0.00 T0	15.00 N N	
26	BP	7104	28/01/2018	DD	Premises Insurance	0	55.00	0.00 T0	55.00 N N	
					Totals £		3,269.08	143.82	3,412.90	

Evidence 5 – Audit Trail

Date:	18/01/2018					How Two Ltd.							Page:
Time:	20:54:40					Audit Trail (Detailed)							

Date From:	01/01/2018	Customer From:	
Date To:	31/01/2018	Customer To:	ZZZZZZZZ
Transaction From:	1	Supplier From:	
Transaction To:	99,999,999	Supplier To:	ZZZZZZZZ
Exclude Deleted Tran:	No		

No	Type	A/C	N/C	Dept	Details	Date	Ref	Net	Tax	T/C	Pd	Paid	V	B	Bank Rec. Date
1	JD	0030				01/01/2018	O/Bal	7,840.00	0.00		Y	7,840.00	-		
		1	0030	0	Opening Balance			7,840.00	0.00	T9		7,840.00	-		
2	JC	9998				01/01/2018	O/Bal	7,840.00	0.00		Y	7,840.00	-		
		2	9998	0	Opening Balance			7,840.00	0.00	T9		7,840.00	-		
3	JD	0050				01/01/2018	O/Bal	12,370.00	0.00		Y	12,370.00	-		
		3	0050	0	Opening Balance			12,370.00	0.00	T9		12,370.00	-		
4	JC	9998				01/01/2018	O/Bal	12,370.00	0.00		Y	12,370.00	-		
		4	9998	0	Opening Balance			12,370.00	0.00	T9		12,370.00	-		
5	JD	1200				01/01/2018	O/Bal	3,745.00	0.00		Y	3,745.00	-		31/12/2018
		5	1200	0	Opening Balance			3,745.00	0.00	T9		3,745.00	-		
6	JC	9998				01/01/2018	O/Bal	3,745.00	0.00		Y	3,745.00	-		
		6	9998	0	Opening Balance			3,745.00	0.00	T9		3,745.00	-		
7	JD	1230				01/01/2018	O/Bal	750.00	0.00		Y	750.00	-		31/12/2018
		7	1230	0	Opening Balance			750.00	0.00	T9		750.00	-		
8	JC	9998				01/01/2018	O/Bal	750.00	0.00		Y	750.00	-		
		8	9998	0	Opening Balance			750.00	0.00	T9		750.00	-		
9	JC	2300				01/01/2018	O/Bal	12,500.00	0.00		Y	12,500.00	-		
		9	2300	0	Opening Balance			12,500.00	0.00	T9		12,500.00	-		
10	JD	9998				01/01/2018	O/Bal	12,500.00	0.00		Y	12,500.00	-		
		10	9998	0	Opening Balance			12,500.00	0.00	T9		12,500.00	-		
11	JC	3000				01/01/2018	O/Bal	15,000.00	0.00		Y	15,000.00	-		
		11	3000	0	Opening Balance			15,000.00	0.00	T9		15,000.00	-		
12	JD	9998				01/01/2018	O/Bal	15,000.00	0.00		Y	15,000.00	-		

Date:	18/01/2018					How Two Ltd.							Page:
Time:	20:54:40					Audit Trail (Detailed)							

No	Type	A/C	N/C	Dept	Details	Date	Ref	Net	Tax	T/C	Pd	Paid	V	B	Bank Rec. Date
		12	9998	0	Opening Balance			15,000.00	0.00	T9		15,000.00	-		
13	JD	7004				01/01/2018	O/Bal	2,450.00	0.00		Y	2,450.00	-		
		13	7004	0	Opening Balance			2,450.00	0.00	T9		2,450.00	-		
14	JC	9998				01/01/2018	O/Bal	2,450.00	0.00		Y	2,450.00	-		
		14	9998	0	Opening Balance			2,450.00	0.00	T9		2,450.00	-		
15	JD	7502				01/01/2018	O/Bal	345.00	0.00		Y	345.00	-		
		15	7502	0	Opening Balance			345.00	0.00	T9		345.00	-		
16	JC	9998				01/01/2018	O/Bal	345.00	0.00		Y	345.00	-		
		16	9998	0	Opening Balance			345.00	0.00	T9		345.00	-		
17	BR	1200				03/01/2018	DD	1,500.00	300.00		Y	1,800.00	N		
		17	4000	0	IT Geeks			1,500.00	300.00	T1		1,800.00	N		
18	BR	1200				04/01/2018	Deposit	354.17	70.83		Y	425.00	N		
		18	4001	0	Redshaw Cables			354.17	70.83	T1		425.00	N		
19	BP	1200				06/01/2018	DD	980.00	0.00		Y	980.00	N		
		19	7004	0	Wages			980.00	0.00	T0		980.00	N		
20	BP	1200				09/01/2018		458.33	91.67		Y	550.00	N		
		20	5000	0	PCs R Us			458.33	91.67	T1		550.00	N		
21	BP	1200				10/01/2018	BACS	73.25	14.65		Y	87.90	N		
		21	7502	0	Telephone			73.25	14.65	T1		87.90	N		
22	BP	1200				11/01/2018	FP	1,500.00	0.00		Y	1,500.00	N		
		22	2300	0	Bank Loan			1,500.00	0.00	T0		1,500.00	N		
23	BP	1200				21/01/2018	DD	62.50	12.50		Y	75.00	N		
		23	5001	0	Computer Accessories			62.50	12.50	T1		75.00	N		
24	BP	1200				22/01/2018	DD	125.00	25.00		Y	150.00	N		
		24	7105	0	Computer Insurance			125.00	25.00	T1		150.00	N		
25	BP	1200				24/01/2018	Chgs	15.00	0.00		Y	15.00	N		
		25	7901	0	Bank Charges			15.00	0.00	T0		15.00	N		
26	BP	1200				28/01/2018	DD	55.00	0.00		Y	55.00	N		
		26	7104	0	Premises Insurance			55.00	0.00	T0		55.00	N		

| Date: | 18/01/2018 | | | | | How Two Ltd. | | | | | | | Page: |
| Time: | 20:54:40 | | | | | Audit Trail (Detailed) | | | | | | | |

No	Type	A/C	N/C	Dept	Details	Date	Ref	Net	Tax	T/C	Pd	Paid	V	B	Bank Rec. Date
27	CP	1230				15/01/2018		125.00	25.00		Y	150.00	-		
		27	5001	0	Computer Accessories			125.00	25.00	T1		150.00	N		
28	CP	1230				19/01/2018		199.00	39.80		Y	238.80	-		
		28	5002	0	Printer			199.00	39.80	T1		238.80	N		
29	CP	1230				24/01/2018		45.45	9.09		Y	54.54	-		
		29	7502	0	Telephone			45.45	9.09	T1		54.54	N		
30	CP	1230				27/01/2018		34.80	6.96		Y	41.76	-		
		30	7506	0	Admin Expenses			34.80	6.96	T1		41.76	N		
31	CP	1230				28/01/2018		85.00	17.00		Y	102.00	-		
		31	5002	0	Printer			85.00	17.00	T1		102.00	N		
32	CR	1230				02/01/2018		180.00	36.00		Y	216.00	-		
		32	4000	0	Computer			180.00	36.00	T1		216.00	N		
33	CR	1230				08/01/2018		99.00	19.80		Y	118.80	-		
		33	4002	0	Printer			99.00	19.80	T1		118.80	N		
34	CR	1230				10/01/2018		75.00	15.00		Y	90.00	-		
		34	4002	0	Printer			75.00	15.00	T1		90.00	N		
35	CR	1230				19/01/2018		24.50	4.90		Y	29.40	-		
		35	4001	0	Accessories			24.50	4.90	T1		29.40	N		
36	CR	1230				25/01/2018		165.00	33.00		Y	198.00	-		
		36	4000	0	Computer			165.00	33.00	T1		198.00	N		

2 Mock Assessment 2 Answers

Section 1: Task 1 (20 marks)

Task 1a (5 marks)

Traditional Accounting Software	Cloud Software
No need for an internet connection	Can be paid in monthly instalments with no upfront fees for hardware
All financial information is securely stored on the server	Users of the system can work from anywhere with an internet connection
	Can be synced with your phone or tablet so that you can work on the move

Task 1b (2 marks)

Bespoke accounting software…..	✓
…..can evolve over time to match your changing requirements	✓
…..is available immediately and therefore is more efficient	
…..requires less in house training	
…..is cheaper in comparison to 'off the shelf' software	
…..has no extra per user fees as your business grows	✓

Task 1c (3 marks)

Indicators	✓
Development and installation will only take about two weeks	
Updates are run automatically and are included in the price	✓
Accounting can be done anywhere so long as there is an internet connection	✓
Developed and built to meet your specific needs; it is flexible	
Can be easily modified to match your specific requirements	
Financial information produced is always up to date and current	✓

Task 1d (3 marks)

Definition	Threat
One of the clerks has been processing transactions all day and then they delete them by accident	**Accidental deletion**
You have been working on a project for nearly a month. When you come to work on it again and try to open it, an error message comes up to say that there's something wrong with the file	**Corrupt file**
You have been processing month end adjustments all morning and then your screen freezes and the software shuts down automatically	**Software crashes**

Task 1e (2 marks)

	✓
Give all users of the system a specific way of setting their password so that you can access it on their behalf even if they leave suddenly	
Implement firewalls on all hardware and software	✓
Enlist different levels of access rights depending on the user	✓
Ensure that a backup is taken once a week in case of a fire or flood	

Task 1f (2 marks)

Report	✓
Trial Balance	✓
Aged creditors report	
Profit and loss report	✓
Balance sheet report	

Task 1g (3 marks)

Report	✓
Cash payments analysis	✓
Aged creditors report	✓
Cash receipts analysis	
Balance sheet report	✓
Audit trail	
Sales analysis	

Section 2:

Tasks 2-6 (60 marks)

Evidence 1 – Wedding cakes sales analysis

Date:	18/01/2018				**Cakes Away**				Page:	1
Time:	21:24:17				**Nominal Activity**					

Date From:	01/07/2018	N/C From:	4000
Date To:	31/07/2018	N/C To:	4000

Transaction From:	1
Transaction To:	99,999,999

N/C:	4000		Name:	Sales - Wedding cakes				Account Balance:		1,150.83 CR

No	Type	Date	Account	Ref	Details	Dept	T/C	Value	Debit	Credit	V	B
18	BR	04/07/2018	1200	FP	H Eastwood Wedding Cakes	0	T1	270.83		270.83	N	N
33	CR	08/07/2018	1230		Wedding Cake	0	T1	395.00		395.00	N	-
35	CR	19/07/2018	1230		Wedding Cake	0	T1	485.00		485.00	N	-
							Totals:			1,150.83		
							History Balance:			1,150.83		

Evidence 2 – Cake accessories purchases analysis

Date:	18/01/2018				Cakes Away						Page:	1
Time:	21:27:23				Nominal Activity							

Date From:	01/07/2018						N/C From:	5001				
Date To:	31/07/2018						N/C To:	5001				

Transaction From:	1
Transaction To:	99,999,999

N/C:	5001		Name:	Purchases - Accessories				Account Balance:			108.20 DR

No	Type	Date	Account	Ref	Details	Dept	T/C	Value	Debit	Credit	V	B
23	BP	21/07/2018	1200		Accessories	0	T1	29.15	29.15		N	N
28	CP	19/07/2018	1230		Cake Accessories	0	T1	48.00	48.00		N	-
29	CP	24/07/2018	1230		Cake Toppers	0	T1	31.05	31.05		N	-
							Totals:		108.20			
							History Balance:		108.20			

Evidence 3 – Trial Balance

Date:	18/01/2018	Cakes Away		Page:	1
Time:	21:28:35	Period Trial Balance			

To Period: Month 12, June 2019

N/C	Name	Debit	Credit
0030	Equipment - cost	9,450.75	
0031	Equipment - accumulated depreciation		1,375.60
0050	Motor Vehicles - cost	15,788.90	
0051	Motor Vehicles - accumulated depreciation		4,752.30
1200	Bank Current Account	1,982.89	
1230	Cash Account	1,487.93	
2200	Sales Tax Control Account		276.67
2201		96.10	
2300	Loan		13,500.00
3000	Capital		8,163.00
3010	Drawings	131.00	
4000	Sales - Wedding cakes		1,150.83
4001	Sales - Birthday cakes		127.50
4002	Sales - Cupcakes		105.00
4906	Bank Interest Received		9.74
5000	Purchases - Ingredients	120.09	
5001	Purchases - Accessories	108.20	
7104	Premises Insurance	35.00	
7105	Event Costs	50.00	
7200	Heat and Light	125.40	
7506	Admin Expenses	76.82	
7901	Bank Charges	7.56	
	Totals:	29,460.64	29,460.64

Evidence 4 – Cash payments analysis

Date:	18/01/2018				**Cakes Away**								Page:	1
Time:	21:30:34				**Day Books: Cash Payments (Detailed)**									

Date From:	01/01/1980							Bank From:	1230
DateTo:	31/12/2019							Bank To:	1230

Transaction From:	1		N/C From:	
Transaction To:	99,999,999		N/C To:	99999999

Dept From:	0
Dept To:	999

Bank:	1230		Currency:	Pound Sterling										Bank Rec.
No	Type	N/C	Date	Ref	Details	Dept	Net £	Tax	£ T/C	Gross	£ V	B	Date
27	CP	7105	15/07/2018		Event Pitch	0	50.00	10.00	T1	60.00	N	-	
28	CP	5001	19/07/2018		Cake Accessories	0	48.00	9.60	T1	57.60	N	-	
29	CP	5001	24/07/2018		Cake Toppers	0	31.05	6.21	T1	37.26	N	-	
30	CP	7506	27/07/2018		Admin Expenses	0	76.82	15.36	T1	92.18	N	-	
31	CP	7200	28/07/2018		Heat and Light	0	125.40	25.08	T1	150.48	N	-	
						Totals £	331.27	66.25		397.52			

Evidence 5 – Audit Trail

Date:	18/01/2018				**Cakes Away**									Page:	1
Time:	21:31:51				**Audit Trail (Detailed)**										

Date From:	01/01/1980								Customer From:	
Date To:	31/12/2019								Customer To:	ZZZZZZZ

Transaction From:	1			Supplier From:	
Transaction To:	99,999,999			Supplier To:	ZZZZZZZ

Exclude Deleted Tran:	No

No	Type	A/C	N/C	Dept	Details	Date	Ref	Net	Tax	T/C	Pd	Paid	V	B	Bank Rec. Date
1	JD	0030				01/07/2018	O/Bal	9,450.75	0.00		Y	9,450.75	-		
		1	0030	0	Opening Balance			9,450.75	0.00	T9		9,450.75	-		
2	JC	9998				01/07/2018	O/Bal	9,450.75	0.00		Y	9,450.75	-		
		2	9998	0	Opening Balance			9,450.75	0.00	T9		9,450.75	-		
3	JC	0031				01/07/2018	O/Bal	1,375.60	0.00		Y	1,375.60	-		
		3	0031	0	Opening Balance			1,375.60	0.00	T9		1,375.60	-		
4	JD	9998				01/07/2018	O/Bal	1,375.60	0.00		Y	1,375.60	-		
		4	9998	0	Opening Balance			1,375.60	0.00	T9		1,375.60	-		
5	JD	0050				01/07/2018	O/Bal	15,788.90	0.00		Y	15,788.90	-		
		5	0050	0	Opening Balance			15,788.90	0.00	T9		15,788.90	-		
6	JC	9998				01/07/2018	O/Bal	15,788.90	0.00		Y	15,788.90	-		
		6	9998	0	Opening Balance			15,788.90	0.00	T9		15,788.90	-		
7	JC	0051				01/07/2018	O/Bal	4,752.30	0.00		Y	4,752.30	-		
		7	0051	0	Opening Balance			4,752.30	0.00	T9		4,752.30	-		
8	JD	9998				01/07/2018	O/Bal	4,752.30	0.00		Y	4,752.30	-		
		8	9998	0	Opening Balance			4,752.30	0.00	T9		4,752.30	-		
9	JD	1200				01/07/2018	O/Bal	2,425.80	0.00		Y	2,425.80	-		31/07/2018
		9	1200	0	Opening Balance			2,425.80	0.00	T9		2,425.80	-		
10	JC	9998				01/07/2018	O/Bal	2,425.80	0.00		Y	2,425.80	-		
		10	9998	0	Opening Balance			2,425.80	0.00	T9		2,425.80	-		
11	JD	1230				01/07/2018	O/Bal	625.45	0.00		Y	625.45	-		31/07/2018
		11	1230	0	Opening Balance			625.45	0.00	T9		625.45	-		
12	JC	9998				01/07/2018	O/Bal	625.45	0.00		Y	625.45	-		

Date: 18/01/2018
Time: 21:31:51

Cakes Away
Audit Trail (Detailed)

Page: 2

No	Type	A/C	N/C	Dept	Details	Date	Ref	Net	Tax	T/C	Pd	Paid	V	B	Bank Rec. Date
		12	9998	0	Opening Balance			625.45	0.00	T9		625.45	-		
13	JC	2300				01/07/2018	O/Bal	14,000.00	0.00		Y	14,000.00	-		
		13	2300	0	Opening Balance			14,000.00	0.00	T9		14,000.00	-		
14	JD	9998				01/07/2018	O/Bal	14,000.00	0.00		Y	14,000.00	-		
		14	9998	0	Opening Balance			14,000.00	0.00	T9		14,000.00	-		
15	JC	3000				01/07/2018	O/Bal	8,163.00	0.00		Y	8,163.00	-		
		15	3000	0	Opening Balance			8,163.00	0.00	T9		8,163.00	-		
16	JD	9998				01/07/2018	O/Bal	8,163.00	0.00		Y	8,163.00	-		
		16	9998	0	Opening Balance			8,163.00	0.00	T9		8,163.00	-		
17	BR	1200				03/07/2018	Deposit	62.50	12.50		Y	75.00	N		
		17	4001	0	A Parker Birthday			62.50	12.50	T1		75.00	N		
18	BR	1200				04/07/2018	FP	270.83	54.17		Y	325.00	N		
		18	4000	0	H Eastwood			270.83	54.17	T1		325.00	N		
19	BR	1200				10/07/2018	Int	9.74	0.00		Y	9.74	N		
		19	4906	0	Bank Interest			9.74	0.00	T0		9.74	N		
20	BP	1200				06/07/2018		131.00	0.00		Y	131.00	N		
		20	3010	0	Drawings			131.00	0.00	T0		131.00	N		
21	BP	1200				09/07/2018		63.55	12.71		Y	76.26	N		
		21	5000	0	The Flour Mill			63.55	12.71	T1		76.26	N		
22	BP	1200				11/07/2018		500.00	0.00		Y	500.00	N		
		22	2300	0	Bank Loan			500.00	0.00	T0		500.00	N		
23	BP	1200				21/07/2018		29.15	5.83		Y	34.98	N		
		23	5001	0	Accessories			29.15	5.83	T1		34.98	N		
24	BP	1200				22/07/2018		56.54	11.31		Y	67.85	N		
		24	5000	0	Bake That Cake			56.54	11.31	T1		67.85	N		
25	BP	1200				24/07/2018		7.56	0.00		Y	7.56	N		
		25	7901	0	Bank Charges			7.56	0.00	T0		7.56	N		
26	BP	1200				28/07/2018		35.00	0.00		Y	35.00	N		
		26	7104	0	Premises Insurance			35.00	0.00	T0		35.00	N		

Date: 18/01/2018
Time: 21:31:51

Cakes Away
Audit Trail (Detailed)

Page: 3

No	Type	A/C	N/C	Dept	Details	Date	Ref	Net	Tax	T/C	Pd	Paid	V	B	Bank Rec. Date
27	CP	1230				15/07/2018		50.00	10.00		Y	60.00	-		
		27	7105	0	Event Pitch			50.00	10.00	T1		60.00	N		
28	CP	1230				19/07/2018		48.00	9.60		Y	57.60	-		
		28	5001	0	Cake Accessories			48.00	9.60	T1		57.60	N		
29	CP	1230				24/07/2018		31.05	6.21		Y	37.26	-		
		29	5001	0	Cake Toppers			31.05	6.21	T1		37.26	N		
30	CP	1230				27/07/2018		76.82	15.36		Y	92.18	-		
		30	7506	0	Admin Expenses			76.82	15.36	T1		92.18	N		
31	CP	1230				28/07/2018		125.40	25.08		Y	150.48	-		
		31	7200	0	Heat and Light			125.40	25.08	T1		150.48	N		
32	CR	1230				02/07/2018		65.00	13.00		Y	78.00	-		
		32	4001	0	Birthday Cake			65.00	13.00	T1		78.00	N		
33	CR	1230				08/07/2018		395.00	79.00		Y	474.00	-		
		33	4000	0	Wedding Cake			395.00	79.00	T1		474.00	N		
34	CR	1230				10/07/2018		35.00	7.00		Y	42.00	-		
		34	4002	0	Cupcakes			35.00	7.00	T1		42.00	N		
35	CR	1230				19/07/2018		485.00	97.00		Y	582.00	-		
		35	4000	0	Wedding Cake			485.00	97.00	T1		582.00	N		
36	CR	1230				25/07/2018		70.00	14.00		Y	84.00	-		
		36	4002	0	Cupcakes			70.00	14.00	T1		84.00	N		

INDEX

KAPLAN PUBLISHING